02/2012

Also by John Waters

Shock Value

Trash Trio

Director's Cut

Art—A Sex Book
(cowritten with Bruce Hainley)

CRACKPOT

THE

OBSESSIONS

OF

JOHN
WATERS

SCRIBNER

New York   London   Toronto   Sydney

SCRIBNER
1230 Avenue of the Americas
New York, NY 10020

Permission to reprint lyrics from the song "Pony Time" by D. Covay
and J. Berry from Harvard Music Inc. © 1961 for the world.
Sole selling agent Ivan Mogull Music Corporation, New York, New York.

First Scribner trade paperback edition 2003

SCRIBNER and design are trademarks of Macmillan Library Reference USA, Inc.,
used under license by Simon & Schuster, the publisher of this work.

For information regarding special discounts for bulk purchases,
please contact Simon & Schuster Special Sales at 1-800-456-6798
or business@simonandschuster.com

DESIGNED BY ERICH HOBBING

Manufactured in the United States of America

10 9 8 7 6 5

Library of Congress Cataloging-in-Publication Data

Waters, John, 1946–
  Crackpot : the obsessions of John Waters.—1st Scribner trade pbk. ed.
    p. cm.
  Originally published: New York : Vintage Books, 1987. With additional essays.
  1. American wit and humor. I. Title

PN6165.W38 2003
814'.54—dc21

                                                                2003057304

ISBN-13: 978-0-7432-4627-9
ISBN-10:   0-7432-4627-6

For Pat Moran

Contents

NEW BONUS FEATURES

ACKNOWLEDGMENTS

"John Waters' Tour of L.A." originally appeared in *Rolling Stone*, July 1985, in a slightly different form.

"Whatever Happened to Showmanship?" originally appeared in *American Film*, December 1983, in a slightly different form.

"Hatchet Piece (101 Things I Hate)" originally appeared in *National Lampoon*, November 1985, in a slightly different form.

"The Pia Zadora Story" originally appeared in *American Film*, July–August 1985, in a slightly different form.

"Going to Jail" originally appeared in *American Film*, April 1985, in a slightly different form.

"Why I Love the *National Enquirer*" originally appeared in *Rolling Stone*, October 1985, in a slightly different form.

"'Ladies and Gentlemen . . . the Nicest Kids in Town!'" originally appeared in *Baltimore*, April 1985, in a slightly different form.

"How to Become Famous" originally appeared in *National Lampoon*, May 1985, in a slightly different form.

"Guilty Pleasures" originally appeared in *Film Comment*, August 1983, in a slightly different form.

"Why I Love Christmas" originally appeared in *National Lampoon*, December 1985, in a slightly different form.

"Hail Mary" originally appeared in *American Film*, January 1986, in a slightly different form.

"Celebrity Burnout" originally appeared in *Rolling Stone*, December 1985, in a slightly different form.

"Finally, Footlights on the Fat Girls" originally appeared in *The New York Times*, August 11, 2002, in a slightly different form.

"Catty Corner" originally appeared in *Detour*, August 2000, in a slightly different form.

"Crimes of Fashion: A Look Inside the Criminal Wardrobe" originally appeared in *Details*, June 1991, in a slightly different form.

The Independent Spirit Awards 2001 monologues were originally delivered March 24, 2001, in a slightly different form.

"John Waters Presents: *Boom!*" originally appeared in *Premiere*, April 1996, in a slightly different form.

The Independent Spirit Awards 2002 monologues were originally delivered March 23, 2002, in a slightly different form.

"Stalker" originally appeared as "Crimes of Fashion" in *Allure*, July 1995, in a slightly different form.

The Independent Spirit Awards 2003 monologues were originally delivered March 22, 2003, in a slightly different form.

"If I Were President" originally appeared in *George*, August 2000, in a slightly different form.

Director's Commentary

It's been over fifteen years since *Crackpot* was first published, and I'm proud to say it's never gone out of print. But after rereading it, I realize a lot has changed since I first wrote it. Divine and Edith Massey are dead, Pia Zadora's retired, Patricia Hearst is free and pardoned, and her nightmare is finally over (the Feds owe her an apology, too—she was *always* telling the truth). And, of course, I hadn't made *Hairspray* (the movie) yet, so it wasn't safe to like me. Even the thought of *Hairspray*, the hit Broadway musical, would have been heresy.

Frederick's of Hollywood (p. 4) has now spread to Middle America, Mrs. McMartin and her schoolteacher pals didn't molest anybody (p. 10), and Lana Turner's hairdresser (p. 7) turned against her and wrote a tell-all book immediately after she died. In newly released transcripts of the Nixon White House tapes it's revealed that Diane Linkletter was *not* on LSD when she jumped out of her window (p. 3)—it was all antidrug, Republican, Timothy Leary–bashing hype. And I guess it's finally OK to reveal that the adviser of political affairs for Ronald Reagan (p. 82) who invited me to the White House to discuss exploitation movies was the now deceased but still controversial Lee Atwater.

I've been lucky; some things I wished for in *Crackpot* have come true. Hubert Selby, Jr. (p. 63), *did* write another book, and a magazine (*Artforum*) *does* call me every year and ask for my list of "Ten Best Films" (p. 158). William Castle's auto-biography *Step Right Up! I'm Gonna Scare the Pants Off America* was rereleased (p. 14), and I got to write the introduction and meet his lovely family.

When my favorite Baltimore lesbian stripper, Zorro (p. 75), died recently and I read her obituary in the local paper, I finally had a lead to her past. Like a private detective I located Zorro's daughter in Oregon, and imagine my surprise when she told me she had read what I had written about her mother in *Crackpot* and had already wrapped up a package of vintage publicity stills of her mom to send me in remembrance. Zorro's daughter and I have become friends, and I keep encouraging her to write her own book about her upbringing. I've heard some of these stories, and God, my life seems tame.

Sometimes things I hoped for didn't come true. Even though I predicted that after I turned fifty I'd start drawing my mustache on in blue (p. 73), I still don't have the nerve. I've tried it. It looks good. Maybe I'm just a chicken in the Indian summer of my years.

My "101 Things I Love" and "Hate" (Chapters 6 and 3) aren't always the same anymore, either. I now love brussels sprouts (as long as they're not so overcooked that every vitamin is dead on arrival), yogurt (if it's scarily plain like spackle and no-fat), and I've switched from Vintage Seltzer Water to Evian because Valentino, the fashion designer, told me (with a straight face) that "bubbles make you fat." I *do* wear a seat belt now, because a talented photographer friend of mine was killed in a minor car accident because he wasn't wearing one. And after reading journalist Oriana Fallaci's new book (*The Rage and the Pride*), I think I hate her now rather than love her.

The warden of the prison where I taught (see Chapter 5)

got canned because her parole board released a murderer who did it again (nobody griped about all the killers released who didn't). She later ran a bed-and-breakfast and even wanted me to read a movie script she had written. I guess I got fired along with her, although I still visit my "teacher's pet" (p. 49) who is serving a life sentence or two.

An editor at *Paper* magazine in New York recently pitched me an idea for a television show that could somehow re-create my joyous prison experiences—*Judge John*. If *Judge Judy* can hand out sentences every weekday on TV, why can't I? "Young man," I'd sternly lecture, "you were accused of possession of Ecstasy—a drug that supposedly makes its users love everybody. That sounds like hell to me! Inviting ten people you hate over for dinner? Somebody has to teach drug-users a lesson. Now, you're a nice-looking young fella, but I'm going to have to sentence you to six months home detention . . . at my house . . . nude."

I don't smoke anymore, either. FINALLY! After five packs of King Kools a day for decades (I smoked swimming, in the shower, *as* I ate). Robert Downey, *Sr.*, got me to this weird Beverly Hills no-smoking clinic (now closed) where they gave me a mysterious shot in the neck. (I *ate* my last cigarette before I went in.) My regular doctor later told me after reading the ingredients of the injection in the brochure that none of the medications used had the slightest thing to do with quitting smoking, but somehow it worked.

Or at least for eight years it worked. I don't remember when I had my first cigarette again, but somehow liquor was involved. For the next year I smoked only on Fridays, but at 11:59 P.M. every Thursday night I was waiting to power-smoke a pack. I knew it was time to quit again, and I did. But I accept the fact that I'm never truly safe from nicotine. Any day I could lose control and shove an entire carton up my ass. That's just the way it is when you're a human cigarette.

Here's 70 Reasons Not to Smoke Again:

1. you already beat it once, stupid
2. it poisons you
3. that dizziness when you first light up is really nausea
4. cancer
5. emphysema
6. bad breath
7. bad gums
8. yellow teeth
9. stinking clothes
10. that awful extra package in your pocket
11. stupid matches
12. child-proof lighters
13. money
14. ashtrays; little stink islands for the home
15. being like other addicts I know
16. lack of control
17. guilt
18. it doesn't make you thin anymore
19. withdrawal
20. smelling up other people's houses
21. burning holes in furniture
22. burning holes in great clothes
23. having to go outside and smoke like in bad cigarette ads
24. you can't taste food
25. your car stinks
26. boring others by talking about quitting
27. you can't sit through movies
28. or fly on planes
29. Jesse Helms gets monetary benefits
30. coughing like you have the "croup"
31. health insurance costs more
32. "hotboxing" hurts
33. "French inhaling" hurts more
34. hiding them
35. you keep thinking about it
36. it invades your dreams
37. you notice cigarettes in movies and feel like a slave
38. Aren't you a little old for smoking?
39. awful nicotine gum
40. worse hangovers

41. unsafe driving when you drop a hot ash in your lap
42. I don't *want* to be a Marlboro Man
43. or a Kool Penguin
44. I, an Ashtray
45. fear of coffee or talking on phone
46. tongue odor
47. the packs are hard to open (for me)
48. cigarette machines are so humiliating
49. butts littering your lawn
50. butts on dessert plates are also repulsive
51. a smoking movie director can ruin his own take accidentally
52. you're not a fucking jazz musician, for Christ's sake
53. lighting the wrong end and accidentally inhaling a burned filter
54. smoking butts when you run out
55. yellow fingers
56. car windows are coated with nicotine
57. new cigarette pack graphics suck
58. even if you bum from cute kids these days, they usually smoke awful "Lucky Spirits"
59. infecting your unborn, like crack babies
60. lowering your immune system
61. dentists are appalled when you open your mouth
62. patches are for sea sickness, not smoking
63. even the *thought* of seeing a hypnotist
64. it never ends
65. it makes you lie
66. sex isn't as good
67. even some morons you know *don't* smoke
68. Who wants cigarettes to be the first thought of the day?
69. pitiful smoking lounges in some airports
70. other cigarette smokers want you to fail

• • •

Could I write as politically incorrectly today as I did when this book came out? A "hijacking a plane" joke (p. 12) would certainly be hard to get past an editor these days. "Murdering

Katharine Hepburn" (p. 117)? Oh well, I *still* hate her. Pia Zadora cracking child molesting jokes (p. 36)? I don't think so.

You can see the seeds of my latest movies and other projects all through *Crackpot*. My stringent right-wing fashion belief that white (p. 93) still can NEVER be worn before Memorial Day or after Labor Day turned into a motive for murder in *Serial Mom*. The real-life Baltimore joke shop we called "The Hardy-Har" (p. 70) became the Turnblad family business in *Hairspray*. Fantasizing about "kidnapping a major star" (p. 148) and forcing her "to be in one of your movies" was taken literally in *Cecil B. DeMented*. Joey Heatherton went straight from her legal troubles (p. 159) to the set of *Cry-Baby*, and my obsession with Pia Zadora and Patricia Hearst led to them being cast in my films and becoming friends. The last line (p. 156) of my review of Godard's *Hail Mary* ("Oh, Mary. Hail, Mary.") became Memama's obsession with miracles in *Pecker*. "Why I Love Christmas" (Chapter 12) morphed into my "John Waters' Christmas" monologue, which I've done twice at the Castro Theater in San Francisco.

I wrote *Crackpot* in the mid- to late eighties because I couldn't get a job. Nobody would let me make the sequel to *Pink Flamingos*, and I stupidly wouldn't give up. Since I've always been such a media junkie, I thought I'd try journalism. I hoped I could get a press pass from *Vogue* so I could go to car accidents, bust through the police lines, and shout, "OK, what were they wearing?"

I still occasionally write for magazines when I need an outlet for a fresh obsession, so I've included some new bonus features for this rerelease of *Crackpot*. "Catty Corner" (Bonus Chapter 17) is a kind of sequel to "101 Things I Hate." I'm still touchy about couture ("Stalker"—Bonus Chapter 22). Maybe it's because I broke my shoulder falling off a bike on the photo shoot for *Allure* to illustrate this essay. *The New York Times* wouldn't let me print the word "hair-pie" (Bonus

Chapter 16), so I've replaced the word in this piece about my sudden Broadway hit—just call me Neil Simon with a potty-mouth. Even the Independent Film Channel sometimes tells me I've gone too far (see the rejected Part IV of my 2003 hosting speech about Johnny Knoxville firing the Independent Spirit Award to the winner's table from his rectum).

I'm still a media hag. I never understand when people say they don't have time to read. They're lying. It's easy to have the time; just don't watch television, and live alone. For the record, here are the 118 magazines I get in the mail:

Nest

LA Weekly

Provincetown Arts
   Press

Hollywood Reporter

New York Observer

National Enquirer

Time-Out New York

Time-Out London

Los Angeles
   Magazine

Jet

New Art Examiner

Frontiers

London Review of
   Books

W

Cook's Illustrated

Boston Phoenix

New Republic

Us Weekly

Sunday L.A.
   Times

Sculpture

Star Magazine

Art in America

GQ

Art on Paper

Art & Antiques

Billboard

Vanity Fair

Baltimore
   Messenger

In Style

People

Harvard Gay &
   Lesbian Review

Flash Art

Art Monthly

Art & Auction

The Advocate

Photo

Publishers Weekly

Ocean Drive

Hamptons

Gourmet

Entertainment
   Weekly

Newsweek

Premiere

Gotham

Out

Interview

Cooking Light

New York

Psychotronic

Saveur

Town & Country

Hello!

Provincetown
   Banner

ART Newspaper

Index

Esquire

Elle Decor

Variety

Modern Painters

Aperture

The Villager

Honcho

Globe

Camera Austria

New York Gallery
   Guide

Metropolitan Home

Butt

New York Press

Moviemaker

Nation

Dazed and Confused

Shout

Artforum

Film Comment

The Village Voice

Women's Wear Daily

The New Yorker

Bon Appetit

DNR

Playboy

Video Business

Grand Street

Straight to Hell

Videoscope

Detour

Art Press

Frieze

Coagula Art
   Journal

Unzipped

Blind Spot

Filmmaker

Rolling Stone

Bomb

Boxoffice

Details

Vogue

Daily Variety

Paper

Movieline

IFC/Rant

Flaunt

Sculpture

Another Magazine

Genre

Fangoria

American Photo

Parkett

Spin

ARTnews

The New York
   Review of Books

Adult Video News

Issue

Time

Harper's Bazaar

Purple

Times Literary Sup-
   plement

L'Uomo Vogue

I also read *The Baltimore Sun, The New York Times, New York Post,* New York *Daily News, USA Today, The Washington Post,* and *The Wall Street Journal* every morning. I like to stay informed. And yes, I recycle.

CRACKPOT

1

John Waters' Tour of L.A. (1985)

Los Angeles is everything a great American city should be: rich, hilarious, of questionable taste, and throbbing with fake glamour. I can't think of a better place to vacation—next to Baltimore, of course, where I live most of the time. Since I don't make my home entirely in what the entertainment business considers a "real city" (L.A. or New York), I'm a perpetual tourist, and that's the best way to travel. Nobody gets used to you, you make new friends without having to hear anyone's everyday problems, and you jet back still feeling like a know-it-all.

Flying to L.A. is cheap. Make sure you get a window seat, so you can thrill to the horizon-to-horizon sprawl of this giant suburb and imagine how exciting it would be to see an earthquake while still airborne. In Sensurround yet.

There are millions of places to stay, either cheap or ridiculously opulent, but I recommend the Skyways Hotel (9250 Airport Boulevard), located directly under the landing pattern of every jumbo jet that deafeningly descends into LAX. "The guests complain, but we're used to it," confided the desk clerk on a recent visit.

Once you've checked into Skyways, change into something a little flashier than usual, then step outside your room and glance up at a plane that looks like it could decapitate you. If you're like me and think airplanes are sexy, you might want to

1

plan a romantic picnic on nearby Pershing Drive. It's the closest you can humanly get to the end of the runway, where the giant 747s will scare the living bejesus out of you as they take off, inches over your head. There's even an airport lovers' lane (the 400 block of East Sandpiper Street), where dates with split eardrums cuddle in cars as the sound barrier breaks right before their eyes.

It's time now to rent a car, roll down the windows, and prepare for your first big thrill: the freeways. They're so much fun they should charge admission. Never fret about zigzagging back and forth through six lanes of traffic at high speeds; it erases jet lag in a split second. Turn on the radio to AM— being mainstream is what L.A. is all about. If you hate the Hit Parade of Hell as much as I do, tune in to KRLA, an oldies station that plays *real* music, and listen for "Wild Thing," by the Troggs, which epitomizes everything you're about to see in Southern California.

You're now heading toward Hollywood, like any normal tourist. Breathe in that smog and feel lucky that only in L.A. will you glimpse a green sun or a brown moon. Forget the propaganda you've heard about clean air; demand oxygen you can *see* in all its glorious discoloration. Think of the lucky schoolchildren who get let out of class for smog alerts instead of blizzards. Picture them revving up their parents' car engines in their driveways before a big test the next day.

Turn off the Santa Monica Freeway at La Cienega and drive north. Never look at pedestrians; they're the sad faces of L.A., the ones who had their licenses revoked for driving while impaired. When you cross Beverly Boulevard, glance to the left and you'll see your first example of this city's fine architecture, the Tail O' the Pup, a hot-dog stand shaped exactly like what it sells. Turn left on Sunset Boulevard and take in all the flashy billboards created to stroke producers' egos. Be glad that Lady Bird Johnson lost her campaign to rid the nation's highways of these glittery monuments. Wouldn't you rather look at a giant cutout of Buddy Hackett than some dumb tree?

Proceed immediately to Trousdale Estates, the most nouveau of the nouveau riche neighborhoods. If anyone publishes a parody of *Architectural Digest*, this enclave should make the cover. It's true state-of-the-art bad taste, Southern California style. Every house looks like Trader Vic's. Now climb Hillcrest Drive to the top and shriek in amazement at Villa Rosa, Danny Thomas' garish estate, which boasts more security video cameras than the White House. Stop and gawk and wonder why he's so paranoid. Who on earth would want to assassinate Danny Thomas? It wouldn't even make the front page! Now detour to 590 Arkell Drive for the most outrageous sight of all—a house so overdecorated that it has curtains on the *outside*. Can wall-to-wall carpeting on the lawn be far behind?

When you get to Hollywood, you'll know it—it looks exactly the way you've always imagined, even if you've never seen a photograph. I always head straight for Hollywood Boulevard. Old fogies like Mickey Rooney are always dumping on this little boulevard of broken dreams, calling it a cesspool and demanding a cleanup. But they miss the point. Hollywood is supposed to be trashy, for Lord's sake. It helps to arrive around 6 A.M., so you can see the very small and oh-so-sick band of cultists who gather at Mann's Chinese Theatre (6925 Hollywood Boulevard) to witness Natalie Wood's footprints fill with water as the janitor hoses down the cement. Proceed up the street to the best newsstand in the world, the Universal News Agency (1655 North Las Palmas Avenue), and pick up *This Is Hollywood*, a guidebook that lists all the obvious tourist sights, like Diane Linkletter's suicide leap (8787 Shoreham Drive, sixth floor) and Kim Novak and Sammy

Davis, Jr.'s love nest (780 Tortuoso Way). Further along the boulevard, you might encounter the legless, one-armed white guy who break-dances on the street for horrified families as they stroll up the Walk of Fame. Look around you and see all the real-life Angels (as in the film with the catch line "High-school honor student by day, Hollywood hooker by night") and the David Lee Roth impersonators. Marvel at the fact that Hollywood is the only town where everybody at least *thinks* they're cute.

Frederick's of Hollywood (6608 Hollywood Boulevard), that famous department store for closet hookers, is a must visit, not so much for the polyester imitations of their once-great line, but for a glimpse of their obscure CELEBRITY ROOM. There it was, at the top of the stairs, with a tacky star on the door and a twisted mannequin out front. "What celebrities go in there?" I asked a saleslady, so hard in appearance I'd swear she ate nails for breakfast. "Oh, you know, Liz Taylor," she said with a straight face. "Oh, sure," I thought, realizing I was dealing with a Pinocchio in stilettos. "Can I see the inside?" I pleaded. After much telephoning to various supervisors, I got a grouchy voice on the line that told me, "It's just a room." Finally, a manager, who could only be described as a dame, agreed to usher me in. "What celebrities come here?" I asked again. "None since I've worked here," she said, trying to position her body so I wouldn't see her use a credit card to jimmy open the lock. Finally inside, I felt like a fool. It was nothing more than a nondescript changing room that looked like it hadn't been used in years. Thanking her, I trotted back out to Hollywood Boulevard, feeling slightly more glamorous.

Since Liberace's museum is in Las Vegas, I recommend the next best thing: a visit to the Russ Meyer Museum (3121 Arrow Head Drive; by appointment only). If any director deserves to live so near the famed HOLLYWOOD sign, it's this great auteur. Revered for such movies as *Mudhoney, Common Law Cabin*, and *Vixen!*, featuring female stars with the biggest breasts in the world, Russ is now at work on his $1.5 million ten-hour swan song, *The Breast of Russ Meyer*. Five years in the making, with two more to go, Russ' movie is "an autobiographical film," he said, "with condensed versions of all my twenty-three films, with three ex-wives, five close girlfriends, army buddies, and World War II, the most important part." I think he should rename it *Berlin Alexandertits*.

His museum includes one of the most incredible collections of movie memorabilia I've ever seen. Every wall is covered with astounding posters of all his movies. Volume after volume of leather-bound scrapbooks chronicle his thirty-year career. It's a virtual United Nations of Cleavage. Best yet is the "trophy room." There you'll find a display of memorial plaques, one for each film, listing titles and credits. Props from each set have been imbedded in the plaques. There's Kitten Natividad's douche bag from *Beneath the Valley of the Ultra-Vixens*, a pair of biker sunglasses from *Motor Psycho*, even Tura Satana's famous black-leather glove from *Faster Pussycat! Kill! Kill!*

If you're lucky and a graduate student in Meyerology, the director might take you to the Other Ball (825 East Valley Boulevard, San Gabriel), an "exotic" dancing club where he discovered, and still looks for, buxom beauties. Since the liquor board apparently took away its alcohol license and one of the owners died, the club is not much fun anymore, but those supervixen types are still there and, for what it's worth, totally nude. As we exited, a guy passing by on a motorcycle yelled, "Pervert!" Now, I've been called a pervert before, but it's refreshing to be insulted for looking at nude women.

If you want to go farther "beneath the valley," stop by Maureen of Hollywood (1308 North Wilton Place), the costume designer for many of Russ' later opuses. It's hard to spot—the front window caved in "when the building settled"—but Maureen, a sweet and charming lady, is still there. Gone is her large sign, PROBLEM BRAS, indicating not mastectomy cases but undergarments for women whose "top wasn't consistent with their bottom." Or, as Russ puts it, "She likes to work with tits. She turns out really interesting things, but not in a tasteful way; she's strictly into sheer, bludgeoning exploitation. She's one of the last of the old Hollywood."

If you're looking for celebrities, the easiest one to find is Angelyne. She started her career by erecting giant billboards of herself in Hollywood (corner of Hollywood Boulevard and Highland Avenue), New York, and London, displaying nothing but her likeness and a phone number. Dialing excitedly, I was thrilled that no one answered the first time—the ultimate in Hollywood attitude. Looking like a fifties glamour girl gone berserk, Angelyne drives around town in a hot-pink Corvette, wearing a matching, revealing outfit, blowing kisses to anyone who looks her way. She cheerfully responds to all comments, from "We love you, Angelyne!" to "Yo! Sit on my face!" Although she's making a record, she's currently famous for absolutely nothing.

Angelyne has everything it takes to become a star, but she has one fatal flaw: She has no sense of humor about herself. Every time she is queried about her past, she claims a "lapse of memory" and says her only heroine is "herself." When I asked if she identifies with the great Jayne Mansfield, she blasphemed, "Jayne went into the fourth dimension and copied me and did a lousy job." When she said, "I pride myself that I have more sex appeal with my clothes on than most girls have off," I wondered *who* would be attracted to this female female-impersonator. "I've got no competition" and "I'm very intelligent" were a few of her other humble remarks. Yes, Angelyne is a budding star and a vital part of the Hollywood community, but she desperately needs a new writer.

Of course, when you think about it, *everyone* in L.A. is a star. Idling in my car outside Charo's house (1801 Lexington Road, Beverly Hills), I spotted Charo's plumber, Leroy Bazzarone, pulling away in the company truck (John K. Keefe, Inc., Plumbing and Appliances, 9221 West Olympic Boulevard). Realizing he was more interesting in his own way than Charo, I called the company to get an interview, but I was juggled back and forth between the owner ("Is there any money in this?") and his son ("We're *very* busy!"). It dawned on me that Beverly Hills is the only community in the world where a plumber needs a press agent. After days of phone calls, it struck me that Charo's plumber was harder to meet than Charo *herself*.

Lana Turner's hairdresser, Eric Root (8804 Charleville Boulevard), was much more cooperative. I've been a fan of his ever since reading the *Daily Variety* account of Miss Turner's "rare public Hollywood appearance" at the Artistry in Cinema banquet of the National Film Society, where she "made a dramatic entrance on the arm of her young blond hairdresser." "I think she's an artiste," he told me, explaining that he and Miss Turner travel together but stay in "separate bedrooms, thank you." He does her hair once a week in the salon she had built in her penthouse. "She's got beautiful hair," he said. "I just changed her hairdo; I made it a little fuller. She likes it very close, precise. I softened it up for 'Night of 1000 Stars,' and it went over so well we're keeping it that way for a while." "Are there hairdresser wars?" I asked, wondering if beauticians try to steal celebrity clients from one another. "No," he sniffed, "when we go out together, we *don't* bump into *hairdressers*."

Much more elusive was Annette Funicello's garbageman. If you hang out all Wednesday night, the night she puts out her garbage (16102 Sandy Lane, Encino), you might spot him. His boss graciously declined to give out information, falsely assuming I wanted to look through Annette's cans. As I trembled with fear outside her house, looking over my shoulder for the ARMED SECURITY GUARD CONTROL that a posted notice on her lawn threatens you with, I sadly realized that I had missed the pickup and my chance to meet this mysterious trashman. Oh, well, maybe next trip.

Since visiting celebrity graves is an accepted tourist pastime in Los Angeles, I wanted to pay my last respects to the ultimate movie star, Francis the Talking Mule. Mr. Ed may be all the nostalgic rage these days, but Francis was the true original. Unfortunately, his final resting place is not listed in any guidebook, so the search for Francis had all the earmarks of a snipe hunt.

Most people I contacted laughed in my face. Even Universal's press agents came to a dead end. The Los Angeles SPCA Pet Memorial Park (5068 Old Scandia Lane) hadn't a clue ("But we have Hopalong Cassidy's horse"). The Pet Haven Cemetery-Crematory (18300 South Figueroa Street) had Jerry Lewis' and Ava Gardner's pets' graves, but explained that "a mule would be too large for a crematory." Wiping away a tear, I made a desperate, dreaded call to the California Rendering Company, "Buyer of Butcher Scraps, Fat, Bones" (4133 Bandini Boulevard), and was happy to learn that Francis hadn't ended up in this glue factory. Finally, through the grapevine, I located Donald O'Connor, Francis' onscreen costar. "Knowing the executives at Universal," he said, "they probably ate him. There was only one Francis, but he had a stand-in and three stunt mules. He was kept at the stables at Universal, and I heard he was forty-seven years old when he died. If you find Francis, let me know. We'll make another picture together."

Through the help of the Directors Guild, I found Francis' (*and* Mr. Ed's) great director, Arthur Lubin. Knowing that he had vowed to take the secret of how they made Francis talk with him to the grave, I didn't let on that Donald O'Connor had just spilled the beans. ("It didn't hurt Francis at all," Mr. O'Connor had told me. "They had two fish lines that went under the bridle, one to make him talk, the other to shut him up. There was a piece of lead in his mouth, and he'd try to spew it out. That's what made him move his mouth.") Mr. Lubin admitted that Mr. Ed was the smarter of his superstars ("Let's face it, a mule is dumb"), but relieved my anxiety by informing me that after Francis' career was all washed up ("We made five films; they thought that was enough"), the Humane Society placed him in a good home. Francis died on a nice ranch somewhere in Jerome, Arizona, a dignified star to the end.

San Francisco may be known as the kook capital of the world, but isn't L.A. really more deserving of that much-coveted title? Think of the infamous crimes and colorful villains that have helped give this city its exciting reputation. Take a historical walk down Atrocity Lane and revisit some of the most infamous crime scenes of the century.

Start your day of touring madness by proceeding to Patty Hearst's SLA shoot-out scene (1466 East Fifty-fourth Street) in the heart of Watts. Gone is the charred rubble of the inferno where most of these media guerrillas met their death, but in its place is a spooky vacant lot that seems the perfect resting ground for the misguided rebels. The neighbors call it a "tombstone" and predict no one will ever build on this local battlefield. Across the street at 1447, Mr. Lafayette McAdory will show you his front door, still riddled with bullet holes, souvenirs of the shoot-out. Why hasn't he replaced it? It's "history," he said, waking from a nap on the couch in his garage. Another neighbor told me that the only people he sees snooping around are not tourists but cops, "to show the new ones where it happened."

Feel like going on a field trip? How about a visit to the Spahn Ranch (12000 Santa Susana Pass Road, Chatsworth), home of the most notorious villains of all time, the Charles Manson Family. There is nothing left, "not even a scrap," according to the new owner, but it's still worth the visit, if only to meditate. And if you use your imagination and look up into the mountains, you can still picture this demented Swiss Family Robinson, hiding out, plotting, about to make the cover of *Life* magazine. Make this trip soon, however, because even the grass won't be there much longer. Bulldozers are circling, about to eradicate the last trace of those "fires from hell." And what next? Tract homes? Spahn Acres?

Across the street, the Faith Evangelical Church is, ironically, under construction, and they are "quite well aware" of the situation. "We've had people who say there's a force of evil up there," a secretary told me over the phone. Even Gary Wiessner, the church business administrator, said, "The devil's still up there. I have felt his presence three times: at the Ethiopia-Somalia border, the Uganda border, and at Spahn."

If you want to get really creepy, fast forward to 1985 and start following the McMartin School child-molestation case. It's the talk of L.A. The seven defendants, spanning three generations and charged with 115 counts of abuse and conspiracy, are despised by the public even more than the Manson Family in its heyday. An impartial jury is hard to imagine. The school itself (931 Manhattan Beach Boulevard), once very respectable, now sits like an obscene eyesore, vandalized by the community. The windows have been smashed, and the lawn dug up for evidence. Graffiti—RAY WILL DIE (defendant Raymond Buckey), RAY IS DEAD—echoes the city's lynch-mob attitude. What makes the scene especially macabre is the sight of children's rocking horses swaying in the breeze like props on the closed-down set of some horror flick.

The pretrial hearing (Judge Aviva K. Bobb's chambers,

Municipal Court, Los Angeles Traffic Court, 1945 South Hill Street) is expected to last two years, and it's easy to get a seat. The McMartin defendants must be on hand every day, and they look nothing like the modern-day Frankenstein monsters the prosecutor would have you believe they are. Being open-minded, I had lunch with them. I have no idea if they're guilty or not, but they *do* present their innocence in a convincing way. Even Virginia McMartin, the seventy-seven-year-old matriarch of this clan, had a kind word or two. If you don't hold a cross up to them and scream, they will at least be friendly. After all, isn't lunch with the McMartin defendants more "drop dead" than, say, a lunch with Joan Collins?

Wondering how they could possibly feel, released on bail in their respective communities, I decided to do a little research. I attended a matinee of *The Care Bears Movie* by myself. The ticket seller gave me a funny look, maybe it was my sunglasses. The usher tore my ticket and snapped, "This is a children's movie, you know!" The theater was filled with harried mothers and their kids, many of whom were clutching Cabbage Patch dolls. I was the only adult male by myself and people actually moved away from me. I didn't dare make eye contact. Lasting only twenty minutes or so, I rushed from the theater, filled with anxiety, understanding a little better how Mrs. McMartin and her pals must feel every time they step out of the house.

If your vacation time is running out, there are still a few last-minute sights you may want to squeeze in. Try going to Venice Beach—the only place in Los Angeles that reminds me of the East Coast. Go directly to Muscle Beach (Ocean Front Walk between Eighteenth and Nineteenth avenues), but pay no attention to the pumping-iron showboats who exhibit themselves in a tiny cement arena surrounded by four tiers of tattered bleachers. Concentrate instead on their audience, and experience voyeurism of a new kind. Intently watching another voyeur as he voyeurs an exhibitionist is a thrill you probably won't get to experience at home.

Still feeling kinky? There's a downtown bar that will have to remain anonymous, but if what I heard is true, it sounds very *au courant*. Salvadoran sex changes are the main attraction, and in the spirit of LBJ pointing to his scar, these "girls" will show you their "operations" for $5.

As I finally boarded the plane back to Baltimore, I was so filled with the magic of L.A. I wanted to burst. During take-off, I felt as if I might go insane from happiness over my wonderful vacation. Not wanting anyone to pop my bubble by speaking to me, I immediately began reading *Lesbian Nuns*, and that did the trick. No one attempted small talk. I had six blissful, silent hours remembering the heaven of being a tourist in L.A. I should have hijacked the plane and gone back.

2

Whatever Happened to Showmanship?

Liberace had a word for it. So did *Variety*. The word was "showmanship"—but lately this term seems to have disappeared from movie moguls' vocabulary. After all, with so many bad movies around these days, couldn't the promotional campaigns at least be fun? What's happened to the ludicrous but innovative marketing techniques of yesteryear that used to fool audiences into thinking they were having a good time even if the film stunk? Did the audiences care? Hell, no. They may have hated the picture, but they loved the gimmick, and that's all they ended up remembering anyway.

Who's to follow in the footsteps of the great low-rent Samuel Z. Arkoffs and Joseph E. Levines who used to hype films? Why do today's producers waste untold millions on media junkets, national television spots, and giant print ads when they could come up with something as delightful and effective as handing out vomit bags at horror films? Or how about the high-profile but dirt-cheap antics of the producers of a 1977 redneck oddity entitled *The Worm Eaters*? Realizing that competition for attention from film buyers at the Cannes Film Festival was fierce that year, these ballyhoo experts blithely ate live worms from a bucket as startled distributors filed into their screening.

We can even go way back in history to *Mom and Dad*, a boring pseudo sex documentary from the forties brilliantly hyped by the great-great-grandfather of exploitation, Kroger Babb. Since the film contained footage of an actual birth of a baby, Mr. Babb realized this was a chance to legally show full-frontal female nudity. Did he figure the voyeuristic audience would just ignore the baby and focus on the anatomy? Four-walling a theater in each city, Babb picked up some added pocket change by having a phony nurse hawk sex-education pamphlets in the aisles before the feature began. He assured further controversy by sexually segregating the audience—women only in the afternoon and men only at night. In what has to be the most outlandish publicity stunt in film history, he would start the film and turn off the ventilation. As the audience grew more and more uncomfortable, he would release noxious gas through the air vents and wait for the first person to pass out. Mr. Babb would immediately call an ambulance and the local media at the same time, then rush outside the theater to smugly watch the heavily photographed "rescue of a shocked patron," knowing it would be front-page news the next day.

Without a doubt, the greatest showman of our time was William Castle. King of the Gimmicks, William Castle was my idol. His films made me want to make films. I'm even jealous of his work. In fact, I wish I *were* William Castle.

What's the matter with film buffs these days? How could they be so slow in elevating this ultimate eccentric director-producer to cult status? Isn't it time for a retrospective? A documentary on his life? Some highfalutin critique in *Cahiers du Cinéma*? Isn't it time to get his marvelous autobiography, *Step Right Up! I'm Gonna Scare the Pants Off America*, back in print? Forget Ed Wood. Forget George Romero. William Castle was the best. William Castle was God.

The picture that first put Mr. Castle on the map was *Macabre* (1958). Well, not exactly the picture, but the gimmick. *Macabre* was a rip-off of *Diabolique*, and was filmed in just nine days at a cost of $90,000. Realizing that the finished product was nothing special, Castle came up with an idea that would succeed beyond his wildest dreams. He took out a policy with Lloyd's of London insuring every ticket buyer for $1,000 in case they died from fright. Mock insurance policies appeared in all the newspaper ads. Giant replicas of the actual policy hung over the marquees. Hearses were parked outside the theaters and fake nurses in uniform were paid to stand around the lobbies.

Audiences fell hook, line, and sinker. Nobody talked about the movie, but everyone was eager to see if some jerk would drop dead and collect. Of course, no one died. But if they had, it would have been even better. A death of any kind inside the theater would only have cost Lloyd's of London a paltry $1,000, and think of the hype *that* would have generated!

Mr. Castle got so carried away with the promotion that he arrived in a hearse at some of the premieres and made his entrance popping from a coffin. Was this not the ultimate in auteurism? Would Jean-Luc Godard have gone this far? Would he have arrived in a wrecked car to promote *Weekend*? Would Sergei Eisenstein have arrived in a battleship? I think not. I hate that Sergei Eisenstein.

William Castle was no slacker. Not content to rest on his laurels, he set his feverish little mind to work to come up with what the studios wanted—more gimmicks and higher grosses. His next project was *House on Haunted Hill* (1959), a nifty little horror film boasting the director-producer's first real star, Vincent Price. But even Price was upstaged by Castle's new gimmick, "Emergo." Each theater was equipped with a large black box installed next to the screen. At a designated point in the film, the doors to the box would suddenly fly open and a twelve-foot plastic skeleton would light up and zoom over the audience on a wire to the projection booth. Studio executives were initially skeptical when, at the first sneak preview, the equipment failed and the skeleton jumped its wires and sent a *truly* horrified audience running for cover.

After further testing, Emergo was perfected and installed in theaters all over the country. The kids went wild. They screamed. They hugged their girlfriends. They threw popcorn boxes at the skeleton. Most important, they spent their allowance and made the film a huge hit. Was this not the first film to utilize audience participation to an absurd length? It certainly seemed more fun to me than dressing à la Brad and Janet and throwing rice at the screen during *The Rocky Horror Picture Show*.

Next came *The Tingler* (1959), arguably William Castle's masterpiece. Another horror film, once again featuring Vincent Price, in a command performance. But this time the script had a twist. A Tingler was an organism that lived in everyone's spinal column. A cross between a lobster and a crab, it came to life only when a person was frightened. The only way to kill this little bugger was to scream. In the film, the Tingler breaks loose in a movie theater and kills the projectionist. In real theaters where the film was playing, the screen would go white at this point and a voice would announce, "Attention! The Tingler is loose in this theater. Please scream for your life." Naturally, the audience responded by shrieking their lungs out, but this wasn't good enough for the Master of Gimmicks. He came up with "Percepto," "the newest and most startling screen gimmick." Similar to a handshake buzzer, Percepto was nothing more than little motors installed under theater seats and activated by the projectionist at the exact moment the audience was in a frenzy. As the patrons got their asses buzzed, the theater would erupt in pandemonium. Castle estimated in his autobiography that he buzzed more than 20 million American asses.

Naturally, there were problems. In Philadelphia one beefy

truck driver was so incensed that he ripped his entire seat from the floor and had to be subdued by five ushers. In another city, the management dutifully installed the Percepto equipment the night before the film was scheduled to open. That night the smart-alecky projectionist decided to test the fanny buzzers on a group of older women who were watching *The Nun's Story* on the last night of its run. I'm sure Audrey Hepburn never got such a vocal reaction before or after this "electrifying" screening.

Looking back, *The Tingler* is the fondest moviegoing memory of my youth. I went to see it every day. Since, by the time it came to my neighborhood, only about ten random seats were wired, I would run through the theater searching for the magical buzzers. As I sat there experiencing the miracle of Percepto, I realized that there could be such a thing as Art in the cinema.

I didn't have to wait long for a follow-up. *13 Ghosts* (1960), his next picture, offered "Illusion-O." Each spectator was given a "ghost-viewer," an obscure twist on 3-D glasses. If you looked through the red plastic part, you could see the ghosts; if you looked through the blue, you couldn't. Audiences seemed bewildered by this imperfect technical breakthrough, but still bought the gimmick.

Recently, the Thalia Theater in New York was brave enough to revive the film—on a double bill with Arthur Knight's *The Wild, Wild World of Jayne Mansfield* yet. Imagine my surprise when I entered the theater and was handed a piece of red plastic—the Thalia's own makeshift version of the long-unavailable Illusion-O glasses. Wild with excitement, I took my seat and trembled at the thought of how creative theater management could be. I noticed a few grumpy film purists refusing the ghost-viewer, but they nonetheless legitimized the film, because without any kind of glasses, *13 Ghosts* is still unique—beautifully surreal, almost arty.

Trying to better Alfred Hitchcock's smash 1960 hit, *Psycho*, William Castle unleashed his own transvestite-themed shocker, *Homicidal* (1961). Although some critics howled about cinematic plagiarism, they conveniently overlooked the fact that it was Hitchcock who ripped off Castle first, not vice versa. Forget the shower scene in *Psycho*. What initially attracted the throngs to this "classic" was the stunt of strictly enforcing the "No one will be admitted to the theater after the feature has begun" gimmick. Castle must have reacted to this competition in panic, because he retaliated with a campaign for *Homicidal* so ridiculous and bizarre that many in the industry felt he had gone off the deep end.

Homicidal has the dubious distinction of being the first film in cinematic history to utilize the "Fright Break." Two minutes before the picture ended, the screen would once again go blank and the voice of Castle himself would announce, "This is a Fright Break. You hear that sound? The sound of a heartbeat? It will beat for another sixty-five seconds to allow anyone who is too frightened to see the end of the picture to leave the theater. *You will get your full admission refunded!*" Naturally exhibitors were wary of this campaign because it violated the golden rule of exploitation: *Never* offer a money-back guarantee.

The first time the Fright Break was tested, the entire audience stampeded to the box office and Mr. Castle nearly collapsed. He soon figured out the problem—the audience loved the picture, but the gimmick created such word of mouth that they figured out how to get the last laugh. They simply stayed and saw the film a second time and then tried to cash in. Mr. Castle was no dummy. He began issuing different-colored tickets for each show. It worked. Now about one percent asked for a refund. This one percent seemed to be Castle's ultimate challenge: He went to unheard-of lengths to humiliate the adventurous ticket buyer who had the nerve to ask for his money back.

William Castle simply went nuts. He came up with "Coward's Corner," a yellow cardboard booth, manned by a bewildered theater employee in the lobby. When the Fright Break was announced, and you found that you couldn't take it anymore, you had to leave your seat and, in front of the entire audience, follow yellow footsteps up the aisle, bathed in a yellow light. Before you reached Coward's Corner, you crossed yellow lines with the stenciled message: "Cowards Keep Walking." You passed a nurse (in a yellow uniform? . . . I wonder), who would offer a blood-pressure test. All the while a recording was blaring, *Watch the chicken! Watch him shiver in Coward's Corner!* As the audience howled, you had to go through one final indignity—at Coward's Corner you were forced to sign a yellow card stating, "I am a bona fide coward." Very, very few were masochistic enough to endure this. The one percent refund dribbled away to a zero percent, and I'm sure that in many cities a plant had to be paid to go through this torture. No wonder theater owners balked at booking a William Castle film. It was all just too damn complicated.

Mr. Castle's career as gimmick monger may have reached its zenith at this point, but he kept on going. He used the "Punishment Poll," perhaps his weakest gimmick, to promote his next opus, *Mr. Sardonicus* (1961). On entering the theater, you were given a day-glow card featuring a thumbs-up, thumbs-down design similar to a playing card. Like spectators at the Roman Coliseum, the audience was allowed to decide the fate of the villain. As a (presumably) humiliated usher conducted the Punishment Poll, spectators held up their Mercy/No Mercy verdict to be counted. Not realizing how bloodthirsty audiences really could be, Castle needlessly supplied every print with two endings, just in case. Unfortunately, not *once* did an audience grant mercy, so this one particular part of the film has *never* been seen. Why all this current fuss about the "lost" half hour of *A Star Is Born?* How about the lost footage from *Mr. Sardonicus?* Can't the vaults be searched? Isn't Radio City Music Hall available? Can't something be done to preserve this important footnote to film history?

After *Mr. Sardonicus,* Castle seemed to be suffering from the too-much-of-a-good-thing syndrome. Critics panned his efforts, claiming he was incapable of producing a hit without a gimmick. He tried it again with *13 Frightened Girls* (1963), but all he could come up with was a worldwide talent hunt for the prettiest girl in each of thirteen countries who, when cast, would receive $300, hotel accommodations, and a "first-class" new wardrobe.

Audiences, too, were getting weary of his "Gyro Gearloose" approach to filmmaking. And the moneymen were getting stingy. They gave him their final ultimatum: *No more gimmicks!* But Castle fooled his detractors by apparently acquiescing to their demands with his new film, *Straight-Jacket* (1964), while at the same time employing the biggest gimmick of them all—Joan Crawford. Wisely realizing that all movie stars are merely high-priced gimmicks in themselves, he sent Miss Crawford to the theaters for promotion. Joan got so carried away by being a live, in-person gimmick that she once invited the entire audience to join her for hamburgers in the restaurant next door to the theater, ensuring a riot and front-page coverage. But Mr. Castle was showing his insecurities. At the last minute he panicked and ordered thousands of bloody cardboard axes to be distributed free to his fans.

A great career was limping to a close. The day of the gimmick seemed to be over. His final attempt at horror gimmickry was *I Saw What You Did* (1965), again starring Joan

Crawford. (Castle did go on to produce films like *Rosemary's Baby* and *Bug*, but they are not relevant to this discussion.) The plot concerns teenage pranksters who call random strangers and pant, "I saw what you did." Accidentally, they reach a real murderer, who tries to track them down. At first, the phone company cooperated with Castle's promotion by allowing him to hang huge plastic phones over the marquee. But when teenagers began imitating the script in real life and the phone company was swamped with complaints, Ma Bell showed her usual humor-impaired company policy by refusing to let Castle even mention phones in the ads. Undaunted, he came up with a hastily hatched gimmick, his last and, touchingly, most pathetic. The back three rows of each theater were turned into a special "Shock Section." Longtime fans were disappointed to find that it was nothing more than seat belts on each chair to prevent you from being jolted out from fear. RIP William Castle. You certainly deserve it.

This magnificent career raises some pertinent questions for today. What has happened to showmanship? Is it completely dead? How can we lure people away from the dreaded VCRs, whose sole reason for popularity is that most of us don't have the nerve to masturbate in movie theaters? Sure, some exhibitors have caused a little excitement, but usually by accident. Think of the drive-ins that routinely cause car crashes by unveiling hard-core porno in full view of speeding, merging traffic. Or grind houses (where waiting in line is always scarier than the film itself), which have given new meaning to the term "horror film" by allowing huge rats to stroll about.

The big studios have certainly been no help. Think of that irritating Dolby Sound, which mistakenly assumes that all moviegoers want to become sound mixers. Or the annoying

3-D, brilliantly revived and exploited by Andy Warhol and Paul Morrissey for their *Frankenstein*, and then bludgeoned into the ground by more serious attempts to "perfect" this tired gimmick. Porno, finally, is the only genre to demand the third dimension. Remember *The Stewardesses?* Huge breasts spilling out from the screen. Or *Heavy Equipment?* Gay male porno with, well, life itself gushing into the audience's lap.

The industry as a whole should put on its collective thinking cap and realize that even with today's computer-printout method of filmmaking, there's still room for outlandish showmanship. Stop fooling around and go for broke. The possibilities are endless. Every time an expensive Hollywood bomb opens, theaters could profit by letting the audience in for free and making them pay to get *out*. Show *Inchon* over and over and make a fortune. If your highly self-touted international epic turns out to be boring, why not give out copies of the deal memo that got the thing financed? Think of the yawns that could be stifled when the audience figures out how all this cash was wasted in the first place.

Try variations of the movie-star lookalike contests, but instead of intimidating audiences by forcing them to imitate such impossible classics as Marilyn Monroe or James Dean, pick someone as normal-looking as Jill Clayburgh and let everybody win. Go for community support! Let Mothers Against Drunk Drivers sponsor a car-crash festival—*Death Race 2000, Eat My Dust!* and so on.

All kinds of films could benefit. The producers of *Porky's* et al., pretend their films aren't made for dirty, filthy twelve-year-old lechers, but why not be honest and sponsor a circle-jerk for Cub Scout troops with the winner receiving a call girl for the night? If you want to be civic minded and publicize your newly installed handicap ramps, show *The Crippled Masters*, an honest-to-God karate film with two heroes—one has no arms, the other no legs. Everybody beats them up until one jumps on the other's shoulders, and together they become a killing machine.

If the Edie Sedgwick biopic, *Ciao! Manhattan*, opens weakly, have the top fag hag in each community pretend to OD in the theater and afterward local hamburger shops could sponsor rap sessions on the tragedy of the whole situation.

Even highbrow, critically acclaimed Oscar winners could up their grosses. Drag enthusiastic members of the *Reds* audience before mock Senate hearings in the lobby. Close the concession stand for *Gandhi* and let the patrons get into the spirit of the thing by starving to death.

What's the matter, Hollywood? Are you going to just sit there with your head in the sand? People are getting bored with the theatergoing experience! Can't you come up with something? Will everyone just sit at home with their video machines? William Castle, where are you when we really need you?

3

Hatchet Piece (101 Things I Hate)

I wake up on the wrong side of the bed and smoke my last three cigarettes. I know it's going to be a bad day. My hair hurts. That cloying voice of the FM disc jockey (1) has already gotten on my nerves subconsciously. I smash down the alarm button and realize the very air I breathe is not good enough. I've had it with being nice, understanding, fair and hopeful. I feel like being negative all day. The chip on my shoulder could sink the *QE2*. I've got an attitude problem and nobody better get in my way. Before showering, I kick the furniture. I'm in a bad mood and the whole stupid little world is gonna pay!

I'm not even going to make the bed. The one rotten, suffocating set of polyester sheets (2) I still own is thrown in the garbage. I happily destroy the ozone by spraying on my favorite aerosol deodorant and sneer at the dumbbells who use the nauseating roll-on brands (3), the kind that retain stray underarm hairs from past use to remind you just how imperfect the human body really is. I get the newspaper from outside the door, hoping I'll catch the creep who sometimes steals it (4) when I oversleep, but throw it down in disgust when I see color photos (5) that never reproduce properly and look like 3-D comics without the benefit of glasses. Then the goddamn lightbulb (6) burns out. Does General Electric think I'm made of money? I gotta get out of here. I think I'll just drive around town yelling insults at pedestrians.

On the way down in the elevator, I'm confined with an unattractive neighbor and his slobbering dog (7). I look away, grumbling, knowing that every time you make direct eye contact with these creatures, your IQ drops ten points. I don't see any cats (8), thank God. I assume they're all in other apartments sucking the breath out of babies or, worse yet, in heat, forcing you to use a Q-tip on their private parts to shut them up.

I check the mailbox, but naturally the mail's not there yet. I hate it when the mail is late (9)! Lazy bastard mail carriers are probably reading my postcards and leafing through my magazines at this very minute. At least it's not one of those stupid holidays (10), like Washington's Birthday or Columbus Day, that bring any work you might have scheduled to a screeching halt.

Outside it's hot and muggy. I buy a carton of cigarettes, ever bitter that I'm taxed so highly (11) on the one purchase that actually brings me happiness. They ought to tax yogurt (12); that's what causes cancer. A neighbor, who always seems too familiar for her own good, passes me and makes the mistake of saying, "Good morning." "Shut up!" I snap, making a mental note of her hideous patch-denim maxi skirt (13) and ridiculous ape-drape hairdo (14), so popular with fashion violators. And then I see it, a goddamn ticket on my car, even though the meter (15) has only been in effect ten minutes. I have to take my rage out on someone! I run toward this fashion scofflaw as she gets into the most offensive vehicle known to man, "Le Car" (16), and yank her door open as she frantically tries to lock it. "Not so fast, miss," I bark. "There's a certain matter of this ticket you'll have to take care of—$16 for gross and willful fashion violations!" She gives me the finger and peels out, turning up the radio so I hear the voice of the worst-dressed man in music, Stevie Wonder (17), ringing in my ears.

Glaring at anyone who dares look at me, I get into my own car (an American sedan) and purposely ignore those ridiculous seat belts (18) that make you look so stupid, so overprepared, so paranoid. Who wants to be trapped in an overturned car about ready to explode, fumbling for the buckle? Oh Christ, I need gas! What else can go wrong? I pull into a gas station and, wouldn't you know it, they only have "self-service" (19) pumps. I don't *want* to know how to "fill 'er up," thank you. Humiliated at having to perform this unavoidable task, I see another motorist, who has tried to disguise his bald head by stretching his one remaining strand of hair over his skull in a misguided camouflage attempt (20). Ha! Does he think he fools anybody? "Have a nice day, baldy!" I shout as I sign the credit card slip and hop into my car. Pulling out, I swerve to miss a slightly overweight jogger (21). "It's not working!" I scream at this sweaty hog. I make the mistake of flicking on the radio, but all I can get are those awful talk shows (22) that feature lonely, militantly stupid listeners calling up professionally obnoxious hosts to vent their idiotic opinions. Don't they have friends to bother with their inconsequential views?

I pull up at a red light and am pissed you can't go "left on red" (23). There isn't anybody coming, is there? I do it anyway and just miss a grown man on a bicycle (24) who deserves to get hit for holding up traffic. And then I see it! Something I loathe more than anything—a walkathon (25)! Block after block of dreary dingbats in unattractive athletic outfits, patting themselves on the back for supporting a good cause and blocking my right-of-way. "Hey, stupid," I yell to a yuppie with a Walkman (26), "time is money. You owe me $20 for holding me up." Naturally he doesn't hear me, lost in some awful music, probably that pretentious midget Prince (27). Trapped, I park the car to get a little breakfast. "Join us," says some monster in "camel-toe" slacks (28) as she kisses (in public yet) (29) her lame boyfriend, who has the audacity to wear those awful leather sandals (30) left over from the sixties. "I hope you die," I seethe as I rush to what I *hope* will be a decent restaurant.

But ooooh noooo! It's been gentrified (31), and the first thing I see on somebody's plate is an apple (32). Now, I have *never* eaten an apple. I did take a bite of one once, I'll admit, but I spat it out faster than a snitch turning state's evidence. Do I look like a horse? Don't they have doughnuts or any normal foods, for God's sake? And then it happens. A waiter, I can't help but notice, who is featuring the most offensive shoe known to man, the clog (33), approaches and makes the mistake of actually sitting down at my table and chirping, "Hi, my name is Bill. Can I help you?" (34) Momentarily stunned, I fantasize pulling out a Denver Boot and snapping his ankle to the table leg. "Get up!" I scream. "And what makes you think I want to know your name? I came here to *eat*, not make friends! Just give me eggs and bacon and hold the biography!" He looks pleased as punch when he tells me, "We don't serve meat." Oh, great! A rotten vegetarian (35) restaurant. How could someone *not* eat meat? The waiter's liberal attitude is beginning to cool, I see. He's the type who goes to Chinese restaurants, makes a big deal out of eating with chopsticks (36), and then pompously demands, "Hold the MSG" (37). I wish I could order a huge bowl of red dye #2 from this cretin. "Just the eggs, then," I holler, feeling a snit of royal proportions about to explode.

Sitting at my table, waiting, WAITING for my order, I feel the bile of my rage rising and decide I have to do something. I can't waste valuable bitching time. It's time to call the police and report every single thing that gets on my nerves. They have to listen—it's their job, isn't it? I go to a public phone and prepare to deal with the despised phone company (38). Oh God, it's the old-fashioned dial kind (39), the ones that make MCI impossible. Remembering that I hate MCI (40), too (they sometimes mistakenly charge you for unanswered-ring calls), I move on to more important subjects of contempt. "Yes . . . hello, officer . . . I'm a citizen and I'd like to report the following things that are getting on my nerves: break-dancing in public (41), obnoxious mimes who think they're poignant (42), nude beaches (43), where unattractive exhibitionists insist on baring their sagging bodies, all in the name of health . . . and, oh yes . . . hello? Hello?" I slam down the receiver, enraged that a public servant has dared to hang up on me, and vow to write a letter of complaint later in the day. I get back to my table just in time to see the dreaded "Bill" serving my breakfast.

I start trembling. My eyes feel like they might burst from their sockets. They have dared to put sprouts (44) on my eggs! Oh God! It's not fair. What next? Filthy iceberg lettuce (45), the polyester of greens? Or even worse, obscene brussels sprouts (46)—those little balls of hell, limp and wilted after a lifetime of being pissed on by birds and other contaminated creatures! "I hate you," I say to the startled "Bill" and slam down eight pennies (47), which have no earthly use in today's economy except for insulting waiters.

Maybe I should go to the movies. At least it's dark there. If only I can get there without stabbing someone. I dare to look out my car window, but immediately wish I hadn't. There, in all its naked amateurish glory, is another one of those outdoor "art" murals (48). If this alarming trend can't be nipped in the bud, there'll be an eyesore on every corner. Did they ask ME if I wanted to look at it? How about the poor neighbors who can hardly ignore the public doodling of these no-talents every time they step out of their houses?

Ironically, there's a "No Littering" sign (49) on this very corner. Running to the trunk of my unit, ignoring the blast of horns honking behind me, I retrieve an industrial trash bag from my apartment that I save for just these occasions. Proudly and unashamedly, I dump the contents directly onto the street. Take that, no-littering nitpickers! I feel virtuous, confident that I have created a job. Every time I throw something down, someone will have to be paid to pick it up. It's only common sense.

Cruising along once again in this cesspool known as life, I realize that it is too late to make a detour. I will have to pass the anti-abortion pickets (50) outside of Planned Parenthood. Nothing gets on my nerves more than these pro-lifers. Not even astrology enthusiasts (51), Hermann Hesse (52), or computer games (53). Look at these fools parading up and down! "Mind your own business," I yell. When one of these busybodies (a man, yet) approaches my car with literature, I lose control and scream, "I wish I was a girl so I could get an abortion!" Trembling with rage, I realize I'd better calm down before I get beat up, but can't resist one last taunt—"I hate the pope" (54), I yell to no one in particular.

I have to escape human beings, so I rush into one of those awful twin theaters (55), figuring I can sneak into the other side if this one feature is as awful as I imagine. At least they're not showing boring classics (56), such as *The African Queen* or *The Philadelphia Story*, or, even worse, science fiction (57). I get an overpriced tub of popcorn and forget to tell the lummox behind the snack bar to hold the nuclear butter (58) that ruins a perfectly good snack. I never order a Coke (59), because they smell bad. I take my seat, take one bite, and throw the whole mess on the floor. More jobs. I paid my admission, how dare they ask me to use the trash can? Some short subjects (60) come on, but at least they aren't arty computer films (61) that could drive me to theater vandalism. Where are film censors when we need them? Oh, good. Here come the previews, which they ruin by showing an upcoming film with the most offensive star in the world, Sylvester Stallone (62). I bet he has pimples on his ass. The feature is *Witness* (63), and the two elderly ladies behind me start *talking* (64), of all things. "It's gotten great reviews," one says. "Yes, I bet it will be up for Academy Award nominations," the other opinionates. "Would you SHUT UP!?" I scream as I turn in my seat with a menacing look in my eyes. "You're not in front of your TV, you know," I add smugly. It does the trick. They are so appalled at my outburst that they don't even dare to clear their throats for the next half hour. But as the film unfolds, I begin to wish the entire audience would start screaming. It's about Amish people (65). Why on earth would Hollywood make a film whose heroes are a group of people whose religion forbids them to attend the movies? Halfway through this cinematic abomination, there's an Amish barn-raising scene, backlit with a sunset, that is so nauseating I feel projectile vomiting is a distinct possibility. "Beautiful," says the satisfied ticket buyer to her companion, and I finally reach the breaking point. Leaping from my seat, I rip off her wig, throw it in the aisle, and rush from the theater, screeching vague threats into the darkness.

I hide in the other side of the twin, but not for long. *Mask* (66) is playing. It stars Cher, who was great in *Chastity*, but under the direction of that whining Peter Bogdanovich (67) seems to be getting good reviews for *not* wearing Bob Mackie outfits. It's about a kid with a deformed face who is not only ugly, he's an asshole to boot. His mother is supposed to be a biker, but her Hell's Angels friends are about as threatening as the Seven Dwarfs. Naturally, this Elephant Man, Jr., falls in love with a gorgeous blind girl and, in one scene, tries to tell her how beautiful the sky is. "But I can't see. I don't know blue," she protests. Never at a loss for a sickening solution, Old Ugly heats up rocks to different temperatures, puts them in her hand and says, "*This* is blue!!" "I see it! I see it!"

the girl moans, and I went temporarily insane, slashing six different movie seats with my car keys.

Escaping the theater just before the police arrive, I hop into my car and turn on the radio, hoping to hear news of World War III—anything to get my mind off those films—but instead hear an oldie but baddie by those honky Beatles (68) who ruined rock 'n' roll. It's all too much. How much can one man take? I pull over to the side of the road and start sobbing. Uncontrollably. Please, God (69) (I hate you, too), let me get back to my apartment without being committed.

Maybe I should get out of town. I could go to New York, but I know I'll have a breakdown seeing those liberals ostentatiously holding their ears in the subway station (70) every time a train pulls in. And get into fights with rude cabdrivers who can't even speak English (71). How about the beach? Are you crazy? What would I do, go sailing (72)? Look at convertibles (73)?—those showboat vehicles that scream, "Look at me," and accomplish nothing but making your hair tangled and filthy. I can't even go to the local park for fear of seeing third-rate academicians puffing on pipes (74) and playing the most boring game of all games, chess (75). Maybe I just better go home.

I run from my car to my apartment and double-bolt the lock. I'm shaking, but I'll try to relax. The mail is *finally* here, but it's always a trauma to open it. What makes me think today will be any different? Oh my God! Someone has sent me a dreaded greeting card (76). Can't those stupid relatives ever think of *one* sentence to write instead of running off and giving Hallmark 75¢ for a line that they'll never have the nerve to say out loud? Of course, there are bills. But none so annoying as American Express (77), the worst credit card of all—highest yearly fee that gives you the privilege of an endless supply of junk mail. And, to top it off, you have to pay the *entire* balance every month, so what's the point? All credit card bills stink, because you have to tear off the change-of-mailing-address flap (78) before sealing the envelope, and it's yet another second of your day wasted on forced tasks. I even try to look through a magazine I subscribe to, but immediately toss it aside when I see articles about that big slob, Mr. T (79), who hangs around child-molester trials and poses for pictures, and Bette Davis' fat, Jesus-freak daughter (80), who thinks we'll be scandalized that her mother mistreated her. Ha! It's a wonder she didn't kill her! I notice that one of those nerve-racking subscription cards (81) has fallen into my lap and rip it to shreds, vowing to cancel this magazine, but decide to continue mailing in bill-me-later orders to foul up their subscription department.

I should know better, but I turn on the TV (82), where the dots are too big for proper viewing. I hear a laugh track (83) and actually scream in the privacy of my own home. Frantically switching the dial, I catch the tail end of the news and glimpse the local weatherman (84), the only public-service announcer who, for some unfathomable reason, feels he must act like Bozo to hold my attention. At least it's summer, so he doesn't mention the ridiculous term "wind chill factor" (85), a hype to disguise the fact that the temperature is exactly what you'd expect for that time of year. Must I commit suicide to escape this drivel?

I call a fellow "hater" and he, too, has had an awful day. I make the mistake of asking him if he'd like to go out for a drink. "Are you kidding?" he rants. "We'd probably go to a bar and order a martini and they'd put it in the wrong kind of glass (86). Then some creep with a bi-level haircut (87) would give us a coke-rap (88) on some boring subject like experimental theater (89). "You're right!" I scream, picking up the bitch ball while it's firmly in my court, "where hambones actually go into the audience and try to involve mortified ticket buyers in their nonsense." Continuing on his tangent, my fellow griper starts shouting, "I hate wrestling (90), that one OK sport now ruined by middle-class acceptance, but even more I hate folk music (91), and street fairs (92)." Foaming at the mouth, I drop the phone and, in a frenzy, start hollering so loudly the neighbors begin banging on the walls. "I hate strobe lights (93), rotten performance artists (94), and"— remembering my buddy on the other end—"to be honest, I HATE YOU, TOO!" I know he's hung up on me because I vaguely hear the dial tone in the background of my harangue, but fuck him. Friends (95) are all assholes! I stagger around the apartment, flailing my arms, screeching like a banshee for the whole world to hear. "I'll get you, Jon Voight (96), and you, too, Henry Jaglom (97), and all the other public jackasses who are plotting at this very minute to get on my nerves!" I collapse on the bed, and, to top it off, I get a nosebleed! And I hold directly responsible Bo Derek (98), *The Hobbit* (99), Rod McKuen (100), . . . and . . . gag . . . oh my God, I've actually regurgitated from the mere act of thinking of these subjects. Finally, spent, I manage to fall asleep for a minute or two, but is there any relief? Of course not. I have some stupid dream. But I'll *never* tell you what it was. Because more than *anything* in the whole world, I HATE people who confide, "I had the weirdest dream last night . . ." (101).

4

The Pia Zadora Story (1985)

Pia Zadora is my kind of movie star. She's got balls. You either love her or hate her—indifference is hard to imagine. Even though she's only starred in three motion pictures—the hilariously trashy *Butterfly*, the atrocious *Lonely Lady*, and the soon-to-be-released *Voyage of the Rock Aliens*—she's already earned her star on Hollywood Boulevard in my opinion. She's shorter than Elizabeth Taylor, cuter than Alvin the Chipmunk, richer than Cher, more publicized than Zsa Zsa, and has a better hairdo than Farrah. She may be a national joke to some, but I think Pia Zadora will get the last laugh. I predict she'll be the star of the eighties.

She's taken a *lot* of flack. You see, Pia married well, to put it mildly, and it seems her marriage has received even more attention than her work. Barely seventeen, she wed forty-nine-year-old Meshulam "Rik" Riklis, a multimillionaire corporate tycoon and film producer. His willingness to back his child bride's career seems endless. He owns the Riviera Hotel in Las Vegas; Pia sang there. His company owns Dubonnet Wines; Pia became the girl in the ads. He finances films; Pia stars in them. When she astonished Hollywood by winning the Golden Globe for New Star of the Year for *Butterfly*, there were vague charges that he had somehow "bought" her the award.

What people seem to forget is that although Pia may be an

"overnight sensation," it took her twenty years to get there. She began her showbiz career at age seven on Broadway and has been working ever since. Her credits include *Applause*, *Fiddler on the Roof*, and *Dames at Sea*. So what if she married a rich man? They've been married for over ten years, and by all appearances they certainly seem to love each other. Would she be taken more seriously if she had teamed up with a garbage man? How many people in show business can honestly say they ever *like* their backers, much less *love* them?

Negative reviews seem to slide off Pia's back like discarded mink coats. Who else could retain a sense of humor about herself after sweeping the Razzie Awards as the worst actress two years in a row? Pia rises above it all with a cheeriness that is almost dumbfounding. She believes in herself, and if some of her critics are slow in catching on, then at least they spell her name right. Her enthusiasm is contagious. The press has been kinder lately—after all, the girl's got something or all this outrageous publicity wouldn't have happened in the first place. She can sing, she can dance, and she seems to be having so much fun being Pia Zadora that it's impossible not to like her.

Pia Zadora is the only living movie star that I've ever wanted to interview. I arrived at her press agent's office and was shown a fifteen-minute "product reel" of her new film, *Voyage of the Rock Aliens*. It seemed a perfect vehicle for her, a curious combination of *The Rocky Horror Picture Show*, *Queen of Outer Space*, and the old Annette Funicello beach-party movies. In the taxi, on the way to her Upper East Side co-op, I thought about how I'd kill to have her in one of my own films.

A maid answered the door wearing a Pia Zadora T-shirt and, with no explanation, asked me to remove my shoes. Seeing that the stunning movie-star apartment was not exactly Japanese but high tech to the *nth* degree, I figured Pia was worried the plush carpeting might get soiled. Shown through the apartment, I marveled at the giant glass portrait of a nude Pia in the living room and gawked at her well-equipped gym-workout room. I then entered what can only be described as Pia's "playpen."

Photos of herself as well as, of course, her Golden Globe Award were prominently displayed. Pia jumped up from fooling with her video recorder (she was watching Daffy Duck) and greeted me with a perky kiss on the cheek. She was dressed in a workout-type jump suit and an expensive pair of white boots that still had the price tag on the bottom. When her manager, Tino Barzie, moseyed in and pointed the tag out, Pia giggled, peeled it off, and said, "Well, at least you know they're new shoes." The maid was sent for refreshments and before I could even start the tape recorder, Pia happily revealed that she had just found out she was pregnant. She seemed deliriously happy. I congratulated her and we began.

QUESTION: I want to pay you a compliment, but I don't want you to take it the wrong way. You are my favorite trashy movie actress in the whole world.

ZADORA: Well, *Lonely Lady* wasn't exactly Shakespeare.

QUESTION: Your screen debut was *Santa Claus Conquers the Martians*, right?

ZADORA: Ohhhhhhhhh, God! Can you believe it?

QUESTION: How did you get the part?

ZADORA: I slept with the producer—I was seven years old and he was a child molester. [*Laughs.*] No, I auditioned. As a matter of fact, it was a Joe Levine film—Avco Embassy—the same producer who did *Lonely Lady* did that film and he remembered me.

QUESTION: Maybe they'll do a Pia Zadora film festival and revive *Santa Claus*.

ZADORA: That's what I'm doing now—*Voyage of the Rock Aliens*. It's the sequel to *Santa Claus Conquers the Martians*.

QUESTION: You were a Catholic girl, right?

ZADORA: Still am. The baby's going to be Catholic.

QUESTION: I first saw you in the trailer for *Butterfly*, and I said to my friend, "My God, who is this person?" You looked so wonderfully trampy. That appeal of jailbait.

ZADORA: Exactly. I was lucky because I looked young.

QUESTION: Who was responsible for your image in *Butterfly?*

ZADORA: The director, Matt Cimber. I had no conception of movies or how to do them. Tino Barzie, my manager, knew Matt, who had worked with Frank Sinatra, Jr., and Matt saw this in me, something wild and trashy and campy—it fit a certain bill.

QUESTION: I mean that great pout, that great hairdo. Who did the hair? I want the Pia Zadora Hairdo Story.

ZADORA: José Eber. He's very famous. He's the one who wears the hat and the braid. He did Farrah. My hair was stylized confusion. Every morning you get up, take the drier, mess it up, and that's it. You know, most people slammed *Butterfly*, but it's going gold on video.

QUESTION: Matt Cimber was once married to Jayne Mansfield. Do you feel any parallels to her career?

ZADORA: No. I can't relate to Mansfield or Monroe. The only one I can relate to is Bardot. First of all, there's a certain physical similarity between us. Second of all, she was very strong—she didn't have that affected sexuality.

QUESTION: In *Butterfly*, weren't you nervous about working with Orson Welles?

ZADORA: No. You know, after the film I said to myself, It's a good thing you were so stupid not to be nervous. If I'd been nervous, it would have ruined the whole thing. I went into it with complete confidence. Orson loved his role and he really camped it up.

QUESTION: All the scandal of the Golden Globe—do you regret having won?

ZADORA: Are you kidding? I wouldn't give it back for anything.

QUESTION: But didn't it piss you off? People saying your husband bought it for you?

ZADORA: Sure it did. I almost went on a political campaign. I love to be put on the line. I love a good fight.

QUESTION: There's a rumor that your husband paid the distributor to release *Butterfly*.

ZADORA: No, *Butterfly* was Analysis Films. They begged for that film. They went out of business! They were dumbbells! Twentieth Century–Fox wanted the film, but Matt Cimber said, "No, it's an art film. You've got to have a classy distributor." Analysis did *Caligula* and *My Brilliant Career*. When all that publicity broke, they should have distributed *Butterfly* nationally instead of bicycling it. Nine months later, it comes out in Virginia—who wants to see it? They called and asked for money for promotion. My husband didn't give it to them. On principle.

QUESTION: When did you meet your husband? I mean your marriage is part of your story.

ZADORA: It's part of my aura.

QUESTION: The London *Times* said the way you met your husband was that a friend of your mother's described him to you as the "King of the Jews." Is he, in fact, the King of the Jews?

ZADORA: I can see where they got that from. I was in Otto Preminger's building for an interview, and Rik stopped in and said hello to me, and he was interested. I looked twelve years old. Of course, I had my portfolio with me and I had on these short hot pants. I thought nothing of it, but one night after the show I was in, I got a phone call. He arrived in this big limo, and my mother and I looked from the hotel window and we said, "My God, he's really here!"

At that time I was sixteen and anybody over thirty looked a hundred years old. My mother said, "He's gorgeous. He's great!" My mother fell in love with him before I did. He wanted to take me out, but I was afraid he'd kidnap me. I was young, very naive and career oriented. I was also very smug in many ways—always my own person, independent in the world. Six months went by, and he became kind of a friend. There was a kind of gap in my life when the boys my own age were not mature enough—they were wet behind the ears and I was a career woman—I had been working since I was six years old. My mother's girlfriend who lived in her building in New York found out who he was. She said, "My God. He's the King of the Jews. Bring him up!"

QUESTION: Would your mother have liked him as much if he hadn't come in a limousine?

ZADORA: It's interesting. People say if he wasn't who he was, would you have married him? If he wasn't who he was, he wouldn't be as wealthy as he is today. He wouldn't have that whole aura of conquering.

QUESTION: Did your mother object that he wasn't Catholic?

ZADORA: No. She's very liberal. I didn't convert. He goes to mass with us on Easter and Christmas.

QUESTION: Do you go to Israel with him?

ZADORA: I went to his grandson's Bar Mitzvah with him.

QUESTION: Are you popular in Israel? Are you the rage of the kibbutzim?

ZADORA: Yeah. Very popular. Everyone yelling and screaming. The press is absolutely wild there.

QUESTION: Your husband's kids from his first marriage are older than you. How do you get along with your stepchildren?

ZADORA: Not famously. I don't bake cookies and go over to their houses and watch television.

QUESTION: Isn't it every older woman's nightmare that her husband is going to run off with a Pia Zadora?

ZADORA: He left his first wife way before I met him. I have to say yes—young or old—because *I* feel very threatened when there's someone attractive around. I'm very possessive.

QUESTION: Is it true that your husband is the sixth richest man in the world?

ZADORA: I certainly wish it were. It's far from true. But I'm going to make him work until he is.

QUESTION: I read that he told you you could spend all his money and he would tell you in due time when there wasn't any left.

ZADORA: Everybody always kids me about that. They say, "How much do you spend?" He says, "As long as you keep spending, I'll keep earning," and his tax man says, "Keep her spending, because the more she spends, the more I make."

QUESTION: So you really live the life of *Dynasty*.

ZADORA [*softly*]: In a way, yeah. The thing that bothers most people is that I'm working and I don't have to. He just bought a 727 jet. We have three homes—one in New York, one in Beverly Hills, and one in Malibu.

QUESTION: Your staff?

ZADORA: A secretary, two maids, a chauffeur, a houseman in L.A.

QUESTION: Is there anything he wouldn't buy you?

ZADORA: Oh, I think within reason. Basically he's very much oriented to the dollar because he made it himself.

QUESTION: But if you were without him—is your whole career in itself a vanity production?

ZADORA: First of all, nobody can answer that question. It's like tempting God. What if? What if? It's not that way.

QUESTION: Does your husband allow you to flirt?

ZADORA: Well, I would never flirt. I'm a married woman.

QUESTION: Doesn't your husband own Dubonnet Wines?

ZADORA: Oh, sure.

QUESTION: How did the idea come up for you to be the spokesperson?

ZADORA: His vice president suggested it. It was about five years ago, when I was playing the Riviera and nobody knew who I was. I was the Rula Lenska of wine commercials. Rik said, "No, it's impossible because it's a public company and for her to work and make money for my company is a bad idea." So I donated all my money to charity, but I haven't done the ad since I became Pia Zadora. Then I was Mrs. Riklis. Pia Riklis. Now he's *Mr.* Zadora.

QUESTION: How does he react to that?

ZADORA: He loves it! Do you know what he said when he found out I was pregnant?

QUESTION: What?

ZADORA: He said, "Great, now you'll have someone your own age to play with."

QUESTION: How is having a baby going to change your life?

ZADORA: A great deal. I'm at that point in my life when I'm ready to have a baby. Something real in a crazy world.

QUESTION: Do you worry that people will bring film projects to you hoping your husband will back them?

ZADORA: I'm sure there are a lot of people who do, and he just tells them, "Good-bye, Columbus."

QUESTION: Suppose your husband said, "Quit show business."

ZADORA: In the beginning I did quit—when we got married. I quit for about a year and a half, and I didn't get along in his social circle and I wasn't good at cooking, taking care of the house, and he was the one who forced me to go back.

QUESTION: Before your husband, did you have boyfriends your own age?

ZADORA: Casual. Yeah, one that went on for six or seven years in school. We're still friends.

QUESTION: Were you ever a "fag hag"?

ZADORA: Yeah. I got along very well with gays as friends. I don't know what the real definition is, but I think I was too young to be one. But I was very much involved with the gay community.

QUESTION: Do the mean reviews ever hurt?

ZADORA: Well, it's very difficult to be objective about yourself as a performer. And you've got to read everything. But there's a limit to that—there are certain critiques about myself that have been biased in a certain way: Right away they say, "Well, her husband produced the movie," so right away you know where they're coming from.

QUESTION: How did you feel when *Lonely Lady* swept every award at that "worst" ceremony the day before the Oscars?

ZADORA: I would have hated to be nominated and not won.

QUESTION: But they've written some *really* mean stuff. I'm wondering if you can just laugh it off? Although sometimes a review can be *so* bad that it makes people want to see it.

ZADORA: Exactly. Particularly in the case of *Lonely Lady*.

QUESTION: I was disappointed in that one. I wanted it to be good trash, and it wasn't trashy enough.

ZADORA: You know what was wrong with *Lonely Lady?* It wasn't meant to be trash. It was just so badly done that it looked campy and people thought it was meant to be campy. The guys who made it were really serious. The director has to be the worst director in the history of directors.

QUESTION: Now, Pia, there were some good parts. After you had the lesbian affair, taking a shower in all your clothes because you felt so dirty. That was pretty funny.

ZADORA: But that was intended to be serious!

QUESTION: So why did you do that film?

ZADORA: I did that film because, first of all, it was the only thing I was offered at the time, and I felt audiences weren't ready to see me in *Kramer vs. Kramer.*

QUESTION: It seems as if they purposely made you look unattractive.

ZADORA: The worst hairdresser. The worst makeup.

QUESTION: But you had the spunk to go out and promote it.

ZADORA: I had to, Jesus Christ. If I hadn't gone out, they would have killed me. At least the reviews spared me. Did you read them? They were nice to me: They said, "Poor Pia is stuck in this thing." Nothing could have been worse than it was, from the costumes to the cinematography.

QUESTION: But in your interviews you said it was going to be "great trash."

ZADORA: What am I going to say? It's going to be lousy trash?

QUESTION: Did you like your *Penthouse* and *Oui* spreads?

ZADORA: *Penthouse* I liked.

QUESTION: *Oui* made you look like a four-year-old. Pigtails and that little-girl look.

ZADORA: *Oui* magazine was not exactly a very elegant magazine. *Penthouse* was. What I liked about the pictures was that they weren't blatantly sexual. There was no connotation in my face that it was sexual. It may have been nude, but it was just me—thinking, brushing my hair, character studies.

QUESTION: What went through your head when you were standing there, almost nude, in the fountain at Cannes with 8 million photographers around?

ZADORA: I wasn't nude. I had a backless bathing suit. At that time I was not really communicating with my own emotions. All of a sudden I was in this whirlwind of publicity. I went there with this bathing suit on, never expecting to be swarmed—I'm sure the press people knew what they were doing when they took me out there, but little did I know!

QUESTION: Do you get a lot of scripts offered to you?

ZADORA: I've been getting more recently.

QUESTION: What parts would you like to have?

ZADORA: I would love to have done *Frances*. But I know I couldn't have done it, because I don't look mature enough. I'd like to do *Evita*.

QUESTION: Do you have to go and audition?

ZADORA: I haven't. No.

QUESTION: Would you?

ZADORA: If I wanted the role, why not? Sure, I'll test.

QUESTION: How's the singing career? You won three awards at the Tokyo Music Festival.

ZADORA: I just recorded a duet with Jermaine Jackson—we just came back from Rome, where we shot a video. It's probably the most incredible video that you'll ever see, besides being very controversial, because there's this whole love thing going on between the two of us.

QUESTION: Tell me about your new film, *Voyage of the Rock Aliens*.

ZADORA: It's a spoof. It's very funny. Ruth Gordon is in it. It's pure entertainment. The music is terrific. You'll love it 'cause it's campy. It's the most viable product I've been involved with so far. The most "me" product. Singing and dancing is my background.

QUESTION: Do you get scary fan mail?

ZADORA: No. I've had a few . . . inmates. [*Giggles.*]

QUESTION: How about the practice of sending presents to reporters? I read the *Village Voice* review that ended with, "Hey, Pia, how about a Sony Walkman?"

ZADORA: Right. I sent him a note with a picture, saying, "Eat your heart out." The reason I started sending gifts was that Tino, my manager, said this is what you do. You keep in contact with the press people. Send them a little memento so they remember you.

QUESTION: I think you should do a movie with Liberace.

ZADORA: He was my idol when I was a little girl. I'm Polish, and I played the piano as a child.

QUESTION: You'd be great together.

ZADORA: Oh, God, what kind of an audience would that have? Jeez! Talk about diverse.

QUESTION: I'd love to see you play a killer. Not in a horror film, but *really* a bad girl. What kind of role do you see yourself doing at fifty years old?

ZADORA: Oh, God. I can never see myself at fifty. Give me a break!

POSTSCRIPT (1987)

I will *always* give Pia Zadora a break. *Voyage of the Rock Aliens* was never released in the theaters after all and I can't imagine why. She did, however, have her baby right on schedule, naming the little girl Kady in honor of mom's character in *Butterfly*. Even though Miss Zadora reportedly went through a long, difficult labor, she managed to pull herself together and appear on *Good Morning America* live from the hospital a few hours after the birth.

Today, Pia dismisses her films as embarrassments, even jokingly threatening suicide if *Lonely Lady* is sold to network TV. She horrified her fans by claiming that she might quit making films altogether if she doesn't find the right project. I have one for her, of course, if she'd only take a chance.

Miss Zadora is now a different kind of singer. Forget her revival of Shirley Ellis' "The Clapping Song" ("Three, six, nine, the goose drank wine") that she sang from a moving platform at Studio 54. Her album of pop standards ("The Man That Got Away," "It Had to Be You") delightfully titled

Pia and Phil ("Phil" being the London Philharmonic Orchestra) has hit the charts and I listen to it nearly every day. Her three-month concert tour of America with stops at Carnegie Hall and the Kennedy Center received occasional standing ovations and some great reviews; most notably the tough *Los Angeles Times* jazz critic Leonard Feather, who raved, "Pia's Zadorable. She has it all, the range, expert intonation, a sensitive feeling for lyrics and enough dynamic variety to preclude the danger of overkill. Zadora is nothing to laugh at, and likely never will be again." Even Pia was astounded, confessing she went out and bought ten copies "hoping they wouldn't print a retraction." Pia Zadora is finally getting the respect she deserves. Onward and upward, Pia. I hate to say it, but I told you so, didn't I?

5

Going to Jail

I can't help it, I enjoy the company of murderers, rapists, and child molesters. So I decided to follow my father's advice that "showbiz is never forever" and got my first real job. With a paycheck from the State of Maryland yet. Teaching, of all the peculiar things. Or, in the jargon of the field, "rehabilitating." Criminals. Big ones. Now when strangers approach me to ask about Divine or my next film project, I could truthfully tell them, "Oh, I'm into corrections now." Maybe I can get a job as warden someday.

"Them that can't do, teach," the old expression goes, and I think it's true. In my maturity I realize I don't want to be a murderer, so maybe teaching murderers is the next best thing. A psychiatrist once suggested that if I didn't have the outlet for my rage that my films provide, I might be in prison myself. Who knows? I'm convinced any of us could end up a murderer. It's one career that's never planned. No parents ever raise their children to be killers. Even Charles Manson had other goals as a toddler, I'm sure. Yet even though no one admits it, each and every one of us has in a moment of anger fantasized murdering someone, if only for a split second. Luckily, most people control this urge. What obsesses me are the ones who cannot.

There is no answer to crime (abortion? education?). It happens, that's all. Blame it on original sin or whatever. Before the various vigilante groups so in vogue in every community start to howl, let me say I'm familiar with the victim's side of the story. I've read *Victim* and *The Other Side of Murder*, two devastating accounts of the long-term agony felt by victims of violent crime. Polanski's autobiography *Roman* perhaps best articulates the endless loss and unsuspected ramifications that occur when a loved one is murdered.

But how about the other side of the coin? Can one imagine the equal horror and guilt the parents of the kids in the Manson Family felt? The total lack of community sympathy? The unwanted notoriety? The never-ending feeling that it is somehow their fault? Where do they turn? There is no such group as "Parents of Murderers." I suspect their grief can sometimes be just as strong.

I don't judge criminals. We have judges that are paid to do that. "Ah, but suppose somebody killed or raped *your* mother," you scream. "You'd feel differently." And you know, you're probably right. But no one did, you see. I'm no liberal. Nothing in life is fair. I also bet that if someone in your family committed a violent crime, you'd radically change your opinion on the proper punishment.

"Next time you feel like killing somebody, don't *do* it for God's sake—write about it, draw it, paint it," I advised a startled class of about twenty-five cons the first time I guest-lectured. "These films I make are *my* crimes, only I get paid for them instead of doing time." It was my tryout at the Patuxent Institution, located halfway between Baltimore and Washington, D.C. I was a little nervous, but I felt it was good advice. Maybe a little different from the usual therapy, but practical nevertheless. An old friend, Harvey Alexander, had told me about his job teaching college-credit English courses in the Maryland prison system, and I was immediately interested. When he name-dropped a few of the more notorious local crime figures in his class, I knew I had to go.

Patuxent is the only institution of its kind in the country, and I think it works. The inmates have not been found legally insane, but they might have if they had been able to hire better counsel. All inmates are under full psychiatric treatment and must be accepted into the institution. If the Board of Review feels they are not responding, they are dumped back into the regular prison system. The inmates' violent crimes are sometimes their first offense. The average age is twenty-four, and the prison population is approximately 50 percent murderers, 40 percent sex offenders, and 10 percent what-have-you. Their crimes are real doozies and the average sentence is thirty years. Patuxent even has its own parole board outside the state jurisdiction, and its recidivism rate is much lower than that of other institutions.

Somehow, Harvey had arranged for me to be invited to show *Female Trouble*, a film I made that humorously states, "Crime Is Beauty." After the first of many gates clanked behind me, I lugged my projector across the prison yard wondering how the class would respond. After all, it was 8:30 A.M. and the film was pretty *outré*. Once inside the intricate maze of the prison, I was met by perhaps the most notorious of my future pupils, and he offered to carry my projector. Unbeknownst to him, I had attended his murder trial. I was relieved to have a teacher's pet on the first day.

The classroom wasn't bad. Like all public schools, a little shabby, but then I wasn't expecting UCLA. At least you could chain-smoke. The students filed in and eyed me curiously. They knew I was coming and God knows what they expected. I was shocked at how young they were. Many were white. One looked like my brother. I introduced the film with my standard spiel about trying to make the trashiest film in the world and then the lights dimmed. As the credits rolled, it dawned on me that I was locked in a section of the jail with twenty men society had branded as dangerous criminals and there wasn't a guard in sight. Oh, well, I thought, they seem like nice kids to me; anybody can have a bad day I suppose.

Like all audiences, they laughed most at the sex and violence. Especially if the star, Divine, a three-hundred-pound self-described drag queen with a Mohawk, was involved. Naturally they identified with any scene involving lawyers, trials, or prison, no matter how ridiculously exaggerated. As an onscreen lawyer ludicrously addressed the jury, "If my client isn't insane, who is?" an inmate whispered in my ear, "I wish my lawyer had been that good." When Divine gets electrocuted in the chair at the end, the class became eerily quiet but applauded the credits. As the lights came up, they looked at me differently. Was I a lunatic? I explained my twisted crime theories and they loosened up. They couldn't imagine how I could make my living "on the streets" with this kind of insanity, but they seemed strangely hopeful. I guess they felt: "If *he* can make a living, then there's hope for us all!"

As the class ended, and I was vibrating like a tuning fork from drinking hundreds of cups of tea, the editor of the prison paper asked if he could interview me, and others asked me to come back with more films. I was hooked. For the first time, I felt socially redeeming. As we strolled along the prison corridors, chatting away, past Ping-Pong tables, tiers of cells, and AA meetings toward the lock-down, I was momentarily jolted back down to earth. Behind me I heard one of the students joke, "Hey, somebody's got some sugar in him!" So much for feeling like Johnny Cash live at Folsom Prison.

Harvey was nice enough to ask me back on several occasions and miraculously did the paperwork that passed me through security (one guard staggered me by saying, "Good evening, Mr. Waters. I loved *Pink Flamingos*. Are you going to bring in Divine?") and assigned his class my book *Shock Value* to read. I couldn't imagine how they would react to the chapter dealing with my obsession of going to murder trials that begins, "Everyone looks better under arrest." Could they possibly think that was funny? Was I wrong? Without the glare of the media, they all appeared to be normal. If you could ignore the infamous acts that placed them together, they could pass for an average group of students from a community college anywhere. Except for the homemade tattoos, of course.

I loved going to jail so much it got embarrassing. Overeager, I'd always arrive early and would have to kill time pacing the parking lot under the watchful eye of the guard tower. I was paranoid they might think I had a bomb or something.

In a way I became a make-believe therapist and our class sometimes turned into comic group therapy. Unlike the official doctors in jail, I couldn't judge the inmates and had no say in their getting out. Their attitudes about their prison were sometimes surprising. They didn't really bad-mouth it. They felt for the most part that their therapy was working and they at least had a chance. Many would understandably panic when their shrinks of many years would die or quit and they'd have to start all over again. The clichéd horrors of prison were soft-pedaled—racial tension was not a huge problem and violence was nowhere near as bad as in the jails they originally came from. They had good words for many in the administration—a real rarity in prison patter.

Most admitted homosexual rape was their biggest fear in entering any institution, but they soon realized that at Patuxent it was rare. Sexually, I never figured them out. They joked constantly among themselves about "fags" ("Hey, homeboy, gimme some face") and obviously discussed their feelings on the subject with their doctors. Finally, it seemed no big deal. The administration's position was "homosexuality is not discouraged, since it frequently is the first loving relationship an inmate may have had." For prisoners it was still a no-no if they had to go on the record, but who really cared what happened when the lights went down? If there were any jailhouse sweethearts in my class, I never noticed. I must admit, however, the mistletoe wittily hung over the communal restroom at Christmastime did stop me in my tracks.

Why would you purposely make a film so terrible?" asked a bewildered con after *Pink Flamingos* had been screened, echoing a question my own parents had been posing for decades. The "happy" ending of Divine munching a dog grumpy had just flashed off the screen and, oddly, every black in the class had jumped from his seat and run from the room, never to return that day.

Pink Flamingos as therapy? The very film *Variety* called "surely one of the most vile, stupid and repulsive films ever made"? Before you leap from your armchair to call your congressman, remember that this film is ultimately comedy. If you can laugh at the worst fears of your psyche, isn't that actually healthy? Isn't laughter the first step in ridding yourself of anxiety? Couldn't the film be actual shock therapy? Society's outlaws freaking out over comic situations that positively pale next to their own real-life crimes? The machoest of the macho realizing that humor could be a much deadlier weapon than their Saturday night specials and carry no jail sentence whatsoever?

Harvey and I tried to get them to fantasize about what kind of script they could write on their own. We talked of a prison comedy, one that would concentrate on the ridiculousness of their situation rather than on the horror. Go for humor in a decidedly unfunny atmosphere. One student suggested the title *Reckless Eyeballs*—a term I had never heard. I soon learned it was an all-purpose jailhouse charge used by guards to write up a "beef" on a prisoner's "jacket" when no other charge would stick. "Reckless Eyeballs" simply means giving some-body a dirty look or having a bad attitude, and all prisoners think it a bum rap. I could identify, because almost every person I know on the outside has a permanent case of reckless eyeballs and gives them daily.

Each student came up with ideas for the screenplay: a fat inmate botching up an escape attempt by getting stuck in the tunnel under the fence; a parody of *Scared Straight*, with cons patiently explaining how to commit crimes to a group of innocent junior high school students; a joke on the public's misconception of country-club prisons, with inmates in starched tennis outfits, eating gourmet meals and attending polo matches in the yard. *Reckless Eyeballs* became a fantasy project for us all, one that we knew would never be made, but an idea that kept us going.

The last day of the semester was approaching quickly. We had screened *Polyester* with good results; the irony of con-victs sniffing the smell of dirty tennis shoes from their scratch 'n' sniff "Odorama" cards for college credit was lost on no one. I was still a "closet" teacher, coming in every so often for Harvey's class, and the administration was obviously not uptight. The interview I had done with the prison paper, the *Progressive News*, had come out and the inmate editor told me copies were routinely sent to the governor, congressmen, and other state officials. I hoped they understood the prisoner's humor in the illustration accompanying the articles: a large mock wanted poster with a picture of me and my projector demanding information leading to my "arrest and conviction for the crime of bad taste." In bold letters it joked: "*Subject is armed* . . . with satirical wit *and considered dangerous* . . . to mid-dle-class values. *Approach with caution* . . . or you, too, may be touched. *Shoot to kill* . . . before it spreads."

I was presented with a Certificate of Award that Harvey and the students had been secretly planning. I felt like *Queen for a Day, This Is Your Life,* and the Oscar and Emmy all rolled into one. "This certifies," it read, "that John Waters is owed a debt of gratitude by the undersigned inmates at Patuxent Institution for his taking the time and trouble to meet with us and show us his films during the year of our Lord 1983. Truly an object lesson in Bad Taste." Below, each student had signed his name, crime, and sentence. Since I had known it was bad prison etiquette to ask an inmate what his crime was, I learned for the first time what many of their offenses actually were. The Hit Parade of Mortal Sins was staggering: rape, thirty years; murder, life; armed robbery, thirty-five years; assault with attempt to murder with handgun, fifty-five years; and on and on. Collectively my class of twenty was serving 450 years plus two lifetimes. I thanked them profusely, and when I returned home, I tried to think of an appropriate gesture in return. I could never top their farewell gift, but I did end up sending each inmate a set of postcards showing outlandish scenes from my films and, as a final token of friendship, a photocopied "Get Out of Jail Free" card.

All that was left was graduation day. A real one, complete with caps and gowns, valedictorian speech, noted dignitaries (state's attorney, congressmen), and even a letter from Fritz Mondale's wife, read aloud, congratulating the graduates. All in hundred-degree temperatures in the prison yard. I couldn't imagine what it would be like to receive your college diploma and then go back to your cell to serve your time, but the prisoners seemed festive enough.

Since inmates' families and friends were allowed to bring in charcoal grills and all the supplies for a picnic, I got to meet many of the wives, parents, and children of my students. All were proud. As I munched a hot dog with one of my better students and his family, the father was busy being a host and cleaning up the picnic mess. The student was telling his father how well he was doing, how rehabilitated he was, and how he planned to help renovate the family home when he was paroled. As the father began to reach for his son's soiled paper plate, he asked, "Are you finished?" In confused candor, the son stammered, "What? . . . Killing people or eating?"

Over the summer, I missed prison. I wanted to go back and I wanted it to be official. Harvey and I felt we complemented each other in the classroom, a sort of Laurel and Hardy for the prison set, and we wanted a class that could go further. I had briefly met the warden at graduation, an impressive and attractive woman in her forties who belied the hackneyed cliché of female authority popularized by such great movies as *The Big Doll House* and *Caged Heat.* Although I knew she was deadly serious about her job, I had heard she had been a hit on the television show *20/20* when the institution had been featured, and I suspected she had a good sense of humor. Harvey and I called her to pitch our projects and she set up a meeting with us that would also include the head of education and the chief staff psychiatrist.

Immediately put at ease by the warden's secretary, who had a great hairdo and seemed sent straight from Central Casting, we were ushered in. I soon learned that the warden's first fear was that I might be interested in making a *Titicut Follies*–type documentary on the prison. I was really glad that she knew of this obscure early Frederick Wiseman film, one that had been partially banned due to its harrowing picture of the conditions in a Massachusetts state prison for the criminally insane. I immediately explained that this was the furthest thing from my mind because I thought Patuxent was doing a great job—all I wanted to expose was the good stuff. I handed her a petition from about thirty students who wanted this course to happen. She scanned the list and commented that many of the signers had committed the most heinous crimes but had the highest IQs in the prison. Then we discovered that both of us had the William Morris Agency handling part of our careers.

The psychiatrist, admitting that "gallows humor" abounded behind prison walls, was concerned that my views could possibly be bad for inmates' therapy. I knew what he meant and had wrestled with this question privately. Whenever the prisoners had tried to shock me, I had tried not to react. "Who's your favorite new killer?" one asked, and I purposely downplayed my response. Another student smuggled me a paper done anonymously by someone outside the class. It was a sickeningly graphic account of rape and humiliation written with obvious relish. Not wanting to encourage this individual in any way, I had written across the top, "Some fantasies are better left unfulfilled," and sent it back. With a clear conscience, I told the doctor I knew where to draw the line.

The head of education explained that the institution's video equipment could be made available to us. We agreed that any tapes produced would remain the property of Patuxent and never be allowed out. He suggested how the class could be set up and gave us leads as to who to contact at the Community College of Baltimore, the sponsor of the educational program.

Since my own alma mater had booted me out five minutes into freshman year, I wondered if it was possible for me to get a real, live teaching job. But after meeting with the head of practically every department at the college, I realized everybody wanted the course to happen and it was just the red tape that had to be ironed out. The dean tactfully asked the Patuxent representatives, "Are you . . . well, no offense, John . . . but are you aware of the . . . uh . . . controversial nature of his films?" Everyone laughed, and, presto, our course was approved. Finally, I was a state employee. Imagine.

Filling out the paperwork afterward, I was at a loss as to what to put for my supposed college degrees. "Just fill in 'extensive experience,' " I was told, and I was thrilled to realize I was now the proud owner of an instant college education. I couldn't help feeling like the Scarecrow when the Wizard of Oz gave him a brain.

Since I was now "official," I had to go through teacher orientation. If I hadn't already been inside the prison, I would have been horrified. After being photographed for our ID cards (by one of my students, who chuckled when he saw me coming), a few new teachers and myself were taken into a meeting room and told what to expect. We were given a realistic but scary portrait of the "emotionally disturbed" convict population and then told what to do if we were taken hostage. Our host explained that he himself had once been captured in a prison riot, and although he had been released unharmed, another teacher had been permanently injured. He described a code we were supposed to memorize and punch into the telephone if trouble erupted (if you could get to it—I had no idea where the phone was). If that failed and if it looked feasible, we should "fight our way out." Oh, sure. I immediately decided to get a chronic case of Stockholm Syndrome and cooperate with my captors. My fellow instructors seemed to take all this in stride, but I later found out that in the past, others had fled in horror.

I wanted to start our new class off with a bang. I was glad to see many of our old students, who seemed enthusiastic about our "experimental" course, and was happy to meet the new additions (one of whom had tattooed tears falling from his eye). I wondered how they had been mysteriously judged fit for our special brand of rehabilitation. We had decided to screen one of my celluloid atrocities, *Desperate Living*, which may have been a mistake because the head of education (one of our main supporters) had decided to come to the first class. He had never seen my work. As the turgid melodrama of Mortville, a town so awful that criminals could choose to live there rather than go to prison, unfolded, I could see he was shifting in his seat. The inmates, most of whom had seen my other films, responded as usual, but I could tell they were nervously checking out his reaction. When the leading character, Mole, a lesbian who had gotten a sex change, cut off her new penis and threw it out the door and a dog ate it, I thought he might die. "Enjoying it?" wisecracked a con. The educator shook his head and blurted out, "No!" Oh, God, I thought, here it goes—fired the first day.

The discussion that followed was fruitful, although all the inmates said they would rather stay in jail than go to Mortville. "At least we don't have to eat rats," one said. I may have made things worse by giving out my first homework assignment: Each inmate should assume the role of therapist and write a paper analyzing my characters and recommending treatment. "Suicide," one joked, but the papers turned out to be pretty good. "Mole seems to be a manic-depressive with a schizoid overlay combined with extreme homicidal tendencies along with a severe sexual identity crisis," one wrote. As the educator and I walked to the parking lot following the class, he looked hard at me, shrugged, and commented, "I don't know whether to thank you, John, or punch you."

The next week I passed the warden on my way in and she was friendly, so I figured I still had a job. As long as it wasn't a steady diet of my films, I guess it was OK. *Wise Blood* was next on the agenda, and it went over pretty well, although one student commented, "Every week, John, I hope there will be an image in the films that I can masturbate to later, but I never seem to find one." The class wrote reviews of the picture and I sent some of them to the producer, whom I had met briefly. "Only convicts should be allowed to write reviews," he wrote back.

We followed that up with *A Streetcar Named Desire*, which

went over like a lead balloon. "Pitiful" and "corny" were the main adjectives used in critiquing the film. Sorry, Tennessee. Many in the class didn't even show up that day, since *Young Doctors in Love* was screening at the same time in the gym and had received great word of mouth. (I later met the prisoner projectionist, who told me the best reaction to any film he had shown was for *The Champ*, and the worst for *Chariots of Fire*.)

Our last film was *Fat City*, which went over well, especially Susan Tyrrell's performance as a drunken lowlife, but I think by now everyone was getting weary of the "losers" so lovingly depicted in our series. It was time to put on our own little show.

The class really enjoyed seeing themselves on video. We started with improvisation. Each wrote up a situation and put it in a hat; we drew numbers to choose acting partners. Two convicts in a cell, one to be released the next day, the other about to blow up the prison with a homemade bomb (true to life, snitching never came up as a solution); a brother meeting his long-lost sister in a restaurant, only to discover she has had a sex change into a man. ("What happened to your tits?" "Bookends!") Some went even further and wrote specific scenes: a psycho flipping out in his padded cell; a prisoner's last words as he's strapped into the electric chair; a despairing inmate committing suicide. Not all were so depressing: a Cheech and Chong–type routine of two potheads eating the grass as a policeman tails their car; a welfare worker coming on to a startled applicant.

At about this time, *60 Minutes* had the run of the prison to do an investigative piece on the institution. They never saw the class, which was just as well, since our inmates wanted no part of it—they figured viewers might finger them for crimes they didn't commit or hadn't been prosecuted for.

The last day I resisted the requests of some of the students to bring in porno videos, and instead we did mass improvs featuring the entire class on camera: a tent revival led by a berserk preacher, a bratty kindergarten class, and a 747 full of passengers about to crash were the most fun. With fifteen minutes left before the end, someone came up with the best idea of all. Singed into my memory is the image of the biggest brute in the class playing Santa Claus as each con sat on his lap telling what he wanted for Christmas. Ho, ho, ho was never like this.

Weeks later, Harvey and I met over lunch to reflect on our project. Harvey taught in the prisons for a living, so he was hardly a volunteer, but was I guilty of "Junior League work," as a friend suggested? I couldn't help wondering who got more out of the class—me or the prisoners? I didn't want to be a low-rent Truman Capote, exploiting their stories all the while tsk-tsking their crimes. I genuinely liked these people. I'm not saying they shouldn't be in jail. You can't defend their crimes, but then again who *wants* to be a child molester? If they were run-of-the-mill career criminals, I might have felt more distance, but these guys were like many people I knew. I admit it was difficult to connect the face of a student I liked with his crime and force myself to imagine the misery he had caused others, but now that the crime is over, what are you supposed to do with him?

Was I guilty of "treating them differently just because they were convicts," as one of the student's journals wondered? Well, yes. To me their flaw is their mystery. Why did it happen to them and not me? Would I like them if they *hadn't* committed a horrible act? Most of them, yes, but a few, no—their crime was the only thing that made them remarkable.

Harvey and I played parole board. If it was our responsibility, which ones would we release? We surprised each other by saying no to some of the most talented. Oddly enough, we felt the murderers would be the best risk. No matter what, it *was* their first offense. But what can they say to make it up to society? "I believe the only way I can half make up for the lives I've taken is to be a better person," one wrote. "See, these people I killed are a part of me now until I die. I took God's rights in my hands and now I'm responsible for them for the rest of my life." Is any statement enough? Feeling and saying you're sorry over and over for twenty years finally loses its meaning. But suppose the students showed up on our doorsteps? What then, we wondered? Just how far does this job go? I went back for three more years to find out.

6

Puff Piece (101 Things I Love)

I'm so thrilled to be alive that I awake exactly five seconds before my alarm clock is set to ring. All on my own. Like a big boy. I lie there happily remembering the especially scary nightmare (1) I had. Just think, I have all day to be obsessed. I immediately consult my file card (2) I prepared the night before that lists every move of the day in exact order. I can't wait to do things so I can cross them off and feel like I've accomplished something. I slip into my handsomely decorated Kleenex boxes (3) I use as slippers and stomp into the kitchen feeling as eccentric as all get out. If you saw me leaping and hopping across the parquet floors you'd probably think me crazy, but we all know if you step on a crack you break your mother's back so we can't be too careful these days. I glance at my unopened carton of Kool Milds (4) and feel more secure. In the kitchen, I brew my Twinings Prince of Wales Tea (5) and let it steep so long that it actually hurts to drink it. Yummy. It's not a weekend so I don't make my favorite heart-attack breakfast (forty pieces of bacon (6) and a gallon of milk (7)) but I do open my Vitamin B (8) bottle and inhale the glorious odor, making sure I never actually insert a pill into my own plumbing. I read the morning paper (9), praying for even the tiniest update on the Manson Family's (10) rehabilitation so I can add the clipping to my extensive seventeen-year collection stored in a special place in the back of a closet. I listen to Glenn Gould (11) on my component set, and lip-sync along with his insane mumbling and humming in the background of his beautifully relaxing piano concertos. Suddenly I'm distracted by little flicks of light dancing in my vision but I'm not alarmed, it's just one of those silly LSD flashbacks (12) that can make a morning so provocative.

It's time to survey my kingdom and make sure nobody stole anything. Phew, it looks like my books are safe. In the living room, at least, where all my fiction, psychology, plays, and literary biographies are kept. I endlessly rearrange them, sometimes kissing favorite volumes. "Good morning, James Purdy (13)," I chirp, "and you too, Violette Leduc (14), you big lunatic. Hi, Anne Tyler (15), I'm glad you live in Baltimore and hey, Hubert, Mr. Hubert Selby, Jr. (16), how come you haven't written anything lately? Look at James M. Cain (17) or Jim Thompson (18), they were prolific and they didn't always get great reviews either." I have to sit down for a moment to catch my breath when I realize Denton Welch (19) is no longer with us. But I bet Ronald Firbank (20) and Baron Corvo (21) were waiting for him at the end of that long dark tunnel on the other side. "And rest in peace, William Inge (22), why did you have to do it? Jean Rhys (23), Jane Bowles (24), Witold Gombrowicz (25), I miss you too. Flannery O'Connor (26), you're the tops." Anybody who wrote of being so obsessed with collecting chickens that she actually made clothes for them is A-OK with me. She may be famous for later raising peacocks but I'll always imagine her dreaming up *Wise Blood* (27) as she stitched away on evening gowns for her darling little birdies. And oh, God, here's my all-time favorite: Grace Metalious (28), author of the first dirty book I ever read, *Peyton Place* ("Indian summer is like a woman. Ripe, hotly passionate, but fickle . . ."). An overnight success, she blew her royalties on Cadillacs, and extended stays at the

Plaza Hotel, got divorced from her decent husband and drank herself to death. What a gal, that Grace. For inspiration I flip through Freud's (29) *Dora: An Analysis of a Case of Hysteria* and *Three Case Histories* (the Wolfman, the Rat Man, and the Psychotic Dr. Schreber) and wish I was this "gifted" at being neurotic. I get so excited, I start applauding the pages. As a matter of fact, I think I'll pretend I *am* the Psychotic Dr. Schreber for the next ten minutes. Since he believed not only that he was a woman but that he was the wife of God, I at least have a chance to be religious.

I rush into my "den" and head for the miniature electric-chair toy (30) with batteries that shocks you every time you touch it. Ouch! Now, I can browse through my four hundred–plus collection of true crime books (31) topped off by the twenty-volume *Encyclopedia of Crime* (32) I purchased slightly reduced. Here's where I can concentrate on the worst of the human condition. Sometimes I play defense lawyer, and spout off closing arguments saving them from the death penalty. Interested in Mary Bell (33), the eleven-year-old strangler who received a life sentence before she even had the chance to become a teenage juvenile delinquent? How about the creep who ate undigested cereal out of the throats of his dead victims (*The Limits of Sanity*) (34)? Or the guy in England who was so lonely he killed his tricks so he could keep their bodies and have somebody to watch TV with (*Killing for Company*) (35)? I've got them all and you're welcome to borrow as long as you don't take the dust jacket, leave a $100 deposit, call every night to tell me how far you've read, return it within a week, and submit a neatly typed thousand-word book report.

By now, I'm dehydrated from excitement so I charge into the kitchen, making sure before entering that I rotate in place exactly three and a half times for good luck. I open the window and throw out two pennies, make a wish, and head for the refrigerator. I'm completely addicted to water (36). Any kind will do but Vintage Seltzer Water is my choice. So bubbly, so cheap, and so delicious. I stand there sipping and savoring for over ten minutes, thinking of the man I read about who weighed six hundred pounds from drinking "vast amounts of tap water." So far this hasn't happened to me, and I feel so lucky that I consider screaming and simply never stopping. By now, my Kleenex boxes are starting to rub blisters on my feet so I figure it's time to get dressed. Besides, I'm feeling lonely.

But not for long. Good morning, Tina. Up so early, Kim? Your hair looks great, Kathy. "Tina" (37), "Kim" (38), and "Kathy" (39) are my roommates. Some realists may point out that they are merely two-foot-high Farrah Fawcett "you-do-the-hairdos" dolls rescued from thrift shops, but it's hard to tell with the giant bouffants and heavy black liquid eyeliner I make them wear. They've become a joke to all my friends. When I'm out of town, I sometimes return to discover that they've been given black eyes and painted bruises to simulate abuse. The situation has gotten so out of hand that I've received Christmas gifts for them. I've never taken these creatures out of the apartment, but maybe today would be the perfect chance to see if I can walk the streets with one of them without getting beat up. I curl up under my favorite cashmere blanket (40) Divine gave me and read them a story, "Chicken Little" (41). I read it with enthusiasm since for about six months back in 1979 I was convinced I *was* Henny Penny. The sky *was* falling and *I* felt it. Twice. But people changed the subject when I brought it up. Except for "the girls." They understood.

After a quick game of Duck-Duck-Goose (42), I get out some of my favorite toys and we play for a bit, my euphoria almost out of hand. Getting dressed ("Turn your head, Tina!") I let them "hold" my "Candy Filled Bullets" (43), seven to a pack, 59¢. Imagine parents buying these for real live kids and contentedly watching their toddlers munching on fake ammunition—"Eat *all* your spinach and *then* you can eat some bullets." I think I hear Kathy laugh but maybe I'm mistaken. Tying my necktie (44) (the only item of clothing I'm trendy about—I wish they'd change the "in"-width every week so I'd have to buy more), I toss the girls the "Dirty Laundry Candy" (45) that comes displayed in a plastic washing machine. Sugar-coated dirty socks! What a world, what a world! This time I'm *sure* I heard Kathy laugh. Loudly. Fully dressed, I complete my "look" by inserting my favorite handkerchief (46) from the most hilariously "fashionable" shop, Comme des Garçons, in my sports coat breast pocket. Nobody but me can tell that these ridiculously priced handkerchiefs were made on purpose with big holes in the middle of them. They're worth every cent. I laugh so loudly that my fillings hurt and realize it's time to go to work.

But first I need more water. I race down my hallway at a breakneck speed and then slide in my socks past the one-sheet for *The Bad Seed* (47) and a framed portrait of Liberace (48) in his youth. WEEEEEE! Guzzling greedily, I'm momentarily hypnotized by the hanging photo of a grouchy and seemingly constipated Otto Preminger (49), surprised by a Baltimore cameraman as he exited the men's room after an obviously unsuccessful visit. Inspired beyond belief, I get a longer head start and slide back the entire length of my hall, this time gazing to the right and glimpsing in a blur the one-sheet for Sam Fuller's *The Naked Kiss* (50) and a sketch of my dream date, Amy Carter (51).

I'm the happiest in my office (52). I like nothing better than a fresh desk blotter (53), five identical Bic pens (black) (54), and three spanking-clean yellow legal pads (55) (*with* perforated tops). First duty—call the box offices of the theaters in town playing the most embarrassing movies so I can hear the mortified employees say the title. "Yes, what's playing, please?" "*Bloodsucking Freaks*," the underpaid ticket seller responds in irritation. "Could you repeat that?" "I said *Bloodsucking Freaks*, didn't I?" she yells before hanging up. A friend who had at one time worked in a movie theater told me the most embarrassing title of all time to say aloud was the Brazilian film *Eu te Amo*, or in English *I Love You*. Every time people would call and ask "What's playing?" he would have to say *I Love You* and sometimes there would be a deadly silence before the caller would sheepishly respond, "I beg your pardon?" Others weren't so polite; "Fuck you," they'd snarl, thinking the ticket taker was trying to be a smart-ass. "I *hate* you," another quipped before disconnecting politely.

Whenever I'm blocked for ideas, I just look up at my eight-foot bulletin board (56) next to my desk and gaze at all the layers of visual aids I've collected over the years. There's the "I did it for Jodie" bumper sticker (57) someone gave me after stupidly displaying it on his own car. He received three speeding tickets in a week and couldn't understand when he protested his innocence that the cop snarled, "With *that* bumper sticker, you're always speeding in my book." Then I gazed at that great *Las Vegas Sun* wire-photo of a giant ostrich (58), escaped from a zoo chasing a totally bewildered middle-aged woman down the street. Every time I see her horrified expression, the creative juices start to flow.

I've been working on an exhaustive study of *The Films of Randal Kleiser* (59). I expect it to be a two-volume set, totaling over three thousand pages and hope it's published by a very intellectual university press. You may laugh but Randal Kleiser is the perfect Hollywood director. Film-snots may call him a hack and he usually doesn't get rave reviews but his movies make a fortune. His first feature, *Grease* (60), is currently the tenth-biggest moneymaker of all time. *The Blue Lagoon* (61) starred a fake-nude Brooke Shields and a real-nude Christopher Atkins. *Summer Lovers* (62), the ultimate Kleiser work, is an awe-inspiring *ménage-à-trois* love story concerning characters who are all young, rich, nude, and stupid. *Grandview, U.S.A.* (63) is a small-town drama in the best of the *Picnic* (64) tradition that took place mainly at a demolition derby (65). I've met Randal Kleiser and he always accepts my praise with caution. "I never know if you're serious, John." But I am. Deadly serious. I think Randal Kleiser is a genius. I'm just not sure if *he's* serious when he makes these wonderful films. But I think he is; God, I *hope* he is.

Time for lunchie. Nothing is more blissful than a sliced chicken sandwich (66) on white bread with lettuce and mayonnaise. Of course, it has to be *real* chicken, not that disgusting pressed kind that tastes exactly like a P. F. Flyer. Topped off with potato chips (67). Twelve of them to be exact, fresh from the bag. As I eat, I flip through one of the best obscure magazines, *News Media and the Law* (68), and read about all the journalists who might have to go to jail. If I'm feeling especially perky I'll reread *Pyromania* (69), a 1951 textbook on "pathological fire-setting," and fantasize my dream pyromaniac who is so devoted to his obsession that he dresses in stolen firemen's outfits and spends hours in a sexual frenzy sliding up and down a pole he had installed in a secret part of his house. For dessert I munch a Zero bar (70) and, consumed by sugar energy, leap from the table and break into a torrid "Pony" (71). When Chubby croons, "When I say 'cheese' turn to the right, when I say 'halt' turn to the left, now CHEESE, now HALT," you can bet I hit my mark. I've reached a new zenith in ecstasy by now, so I slip into my purple suede, pointy-toe wing tips (72) and decide to go out to share it with the world.

It's fall (73), my favorite season, so I stand in the street feeling the glorious wind (74) and watch all the golden leaves swirl around my feet while I pretend I'm in the credits for

Written on the Wind (75). I've always prayed to see a tornado (76) in person so I check the horizon for any approaching funnels. No such luck today. I click my heels together three times in hopes of magic but then remember my last yearnings for storm damage. When the entire eastern seaboard was riled to panic by the news media over Hurricane Gloria, I was in seventh heaven. Boarding up my windows, buying flashlight batteries and candles, I was prepared for disaster. The next morning I was crushed to see that nothing had happened. "It was a dud," I complained to relieved neighbors as I walked to my car to discover a lamppost had blown over and smashed my windshield. It wasn't even windy; the morning news had talked about how "lucky" we had been that the storm changed direction. But here I was the only hurricane victim in town. What *is* this thing called "karma"?

I trot into the convenience store (77) across the street, popularly known as the "Death Dinette." Everything is locked behind bulletproof glass; toilet paper, Chef Boyardee macaroni, even Spam. When the very nice clerks unlock the case and hand you a small bottle of Prell you almost feel as if you're shopping at Tiffany's. They don't carry water but I check every day just to be sure. As I walk to my car, I always hope I'll pass a stranger who is stricken with Tourette syndrome (78), the uncontrollable urge to shout out obscenities in public. I think I'm a closet Tourette case. I've never actually witnessed an attack but maybe one day my fantasy will come true. I'm walking to my car and pass a little old lady dressed in suit, hat, white gloves, and sensible shoes. Suddenly stricken, she yells for the world to hear, "Eat my big hole, felch-face," and then recovers, "Oh, excuse me. I'm so sorry, I didn't mean it. Please forgive me," and she continues going about her business.

Once in my car, I slip on my prize pair of sunglasses (79), secure that after all, I *am* a movie director. I've worn the same model for years; if they're ever discontinued, I might have to blind myself so I could get away with the only other acceptable kind—blind peoples' sunglasses, similar to Ray Charles'. I stop at the bank money machine (80) sometimes five or six times a day. Deposit $8, withdraw $9. Transfer savings to checking—$12. I'm not pleased that the machine can't spit out change because cigarettes are $1.05 in Baltimore so I have to withdraw $2 and feel penny-foolish. Today I take out $15, feel rich, and the money is already burning a hole in my pocket. I could head for the bookshop, barge into the shipping room, and rip open unopened crates to see if the books I saw advertised in *Publishers Weekly* are out yet. But they would have called if *How the Pope Became Infallible* (81) had come in. That used bookshop *still* hasn't found me *The Making of "The Other Side of Midnight"* (82), so I might as well skip that stop.

I head for the chicest shop in town, Recreation Novelty Company (83), a joke shop better known to local aficionados as "The Hardy-Har." They carry everything. Browsing through the Phoney Baloney chewing gum, stink bombs, whoopie cushions, ice cubes with embedded flies, squirting lapel flowers, fake vomit, and Dog-E-Do (three different kinds), I decide to try a little experiment. Could they possibly carry fake nose boogers? Is it possible they are actually manufactured somewhere? "Excuse me, ma'am," I say to the joke maven who's run the shop for years, "I don't know how to put this gracefully, but do you carry fake snot?" Before she can answer, an old idiot browsing through Silly Putty overhears, snorts up his excess phlegm in his nostrils, and yells, "Here, I got some you can have real cheap!" Not amused, I ignore his misguided attempts at humor and try to continue the serious conversation. "We used to carry it," she says without blinking an eye, "but we haven't had any for years." Mildly disappointed, I instead purchase one of those wind-up hand buzzers (84) and wonder if I'd have the nerve to use it if I shook hands with the head of some big Hollywood studio.

I'd better get home because I'm thirsty, and drinking water is too personal to do anywhere but in the privacy of your own kitchen. Driving along, always obsessed with the "blind spot" (85) in the rearview mirror, I hear a radio ad for the best movie of late, *Godzilla 1985* (86) and feel pleased as punch. Tickled to death. Almost gay. I'm so lucky to be having a happy childhood as an adult. As I enter my building, I think about the only other apartment in the world I'd rather have—the one in Alfred Hitchcock's best film, *Rope* (87). That fake skyline of New York outside the window with the changing lighting is the most magical set in film history. Maybe when I'm rich I could hire Vince, my art director, to construct a similar Baltimore skyline to put outside my own window. My view is pretty good but a fake one would be even better. Come to think of it, I wish my whole life was *trompe l'oeil*.

I don't have time to be cooking all day so I make my favorite quickie dinner: very thinly sliced calf's liver (rare) (88), radish roses (89), and twenty-five celery hearts (with salt) (90). I listen to *Gloria Spencer, World's Largest Gospel Singer* (91), and reread the liner notes on the back of the album for what must be the five-hundredth time: "Gloria stands five feet, three inches and weighs in at 625 pounds. Her sister died weighing 628 and you will hear on this album in one of Gloria's songs, the story of her heavier sister and how it took twenty men to carry the coffin to the cemetery. Gloria has not let this problem of overweight stand in her way of leading a normal happy life. Not long ago she met and married Reverend David Gray. Although he only weighs 135 pounds, they seem to be an ideal couple. Gloria also has the unusual ability to type over a hundred words per minute!!" For dessert, I have another Zero bar, this time frozen. I hope *I'm* not developing a glandular problem.

It's getting late and since I like to get up at the crack of dawn, I hop into my bed and look at the television. Without turning it on, of course. The only reason I have a set was to watch my favorite show, *Lie Detector* (92), starring F. Lee Bailey. Every night celebrity criminals would make guest appearances and try to prove their innocence. Carol Ann Fugate (93) was even on once. Most of the test results would confirm their alibis but the best part was when they didn't. "You liar!" F. Lee would scream to a bewildered and embarrassed con artist. For some reason, they took it off the air. Why, I can't imagine. I even paid a friend to lie in his Nielsen diary and say he watched it every night so the ratings would improve.

I've always wanted to throw a TV out the window and hear it crash seven stories below, but every time I have friends talked into it, they chicken out at the last minute. I keep the set on the off chance they may syndicate the old *$64,000 Question* (94) (the one that was rigged and caused the scandal in the late fifties).

It's about time for beddie-bie so I fix a big mug of Ovaltine (95) (malt flavored) and get under the covers. God, it's been a nice day. Oops, I forgot my prayers. I quickly kneel by the side of my bed, thanking God I was raised Catholic since sex will be better because it will always be dirty. I pray quickly and rather urgently; "Please God (96), don't let John Simon go back to movie reviewing in *New York* magazine in time for my next release, and Lord, could You let me be able to afford a brand-new black Buick and a Xerox machine? And while You're at it, maybe they could discover and publish an unknown Genet (97) novel. And I promise to be good if You let Larry Layton (98) be acquitted at his upcoming People's Temple trial. Is that a deal?" Suddenly impatient, I cry out, "God, if You exist show me some sort of sign!" Lightning (99) cracks outside my window and I feel funny-peculiar. Hopping into my bed, I'm pleasantly surprised that in rapid succession five or six people I love (100) call wondering where I've been all day. I fill them in on my fanatic delights and listen to all the gossip, hoping I can use their real-life experiences somehow in my film script. Hanging up, I feel an inner peace engulf me. I even look forward to getting older (101). After all, I'm a baby-boomer, and there will always be more of us to control public attitudes on aging. Senior citizens will be trendy in the early twenty-first century. I've already decided to start drawing on my mustache in blue after I turn fifty. To soften my image. How I look forward to that day.

7

Singing for Your Supper

When you're unemployable, as I am, you have to think of ways to supplement your income. "Between pictures" is sometimes my occupation. I barely made it through high school, can't type without looking at the keys, have such a low mechanical aptitude that plugging something in is difficult, would get in fistfights if I worked retail, and am a complete wimp at physical labor. Welfare is tempting but you need kids these days. All I can really do is blab. So I immediately wanted to take my act out on the road—join the new vaudeville—the lecture circuit. Put on my tap shoes. Sing for my supper. Move over, Sammy Davis, Jr., I've got to make a living. Vegas, here I come.

I always wanted to play vaudeville ever since I was a teenager and used to hook school regularly to attend the Gayety Burlesque in downtown Baltimore. My real idol was Blaze Starr but she performed at the 2 O'Clock Club, which she owned down the street, and they didn't let underage kids in. Years later I tried to get Blaze (who still lives in Baltimore) to play a part in one of my films. As she was nearly reclusive and hard to contact, I finally located her sister who acts as her agent. "Is there any nudity involved?" she immediately wanted to know. "No," I responded assuredly, considering the fact that Blaze must be in her sixties by now. "Oh, well, she wouldn't be interested then," the sister explained before hanging up quickly. I should have known. Legendary strippers never really retire; they still *have* to show it, even if no one wants to look. I wish everyone in the world was a stripper. Except me, of course.

The Gayety was a real vaudeville house, beautiful to look at, and they let anybody in, no matter how young you were. The show was complete—big-name strippers such as Kim DiMilo, Libby Jones, and Irma the Body; baggy-pants comedians, an orchestra, and burlesque routines that were high art compared to today's "floor work." They weren't allowed to take it *all* off, but ignored this law by removing their G-strings and tying them around their waists so they could quickly put them back on in case of a raid (which did happen regularly and only added to my midweek excitement).

My favorite "exotic dancer" in town was Zorro, a very butch local girl who looked exactly like Victor Mature. She'd stomp around the stage naked after removing her cape and mask, sneer at the audience in pure contempt, and snarl, "What are you lookin' at?" The men loved her for reasons I've never been able to fathom. Given some encouragement, I'm sure Zorro would have loved to carve a *Z* or two on every one of their faces to take home to their wives. Zorro must be in her late forties by now, and I bet every time she's lucky enough to hear the TV show theme song, "Out of the night/When the full moon is bright/Comes a horseman known as Zorro!" she leaps from her velvet recliner somewhere in suburban Baltimore and wildly slices imaginary *Z*s in the air while ripping off her clothes in a frenzy of nostalgia.

In between acts at some of the strip houses, they routinely showed "nudist camp" pictures, and I was profoundly influenced. Since every other type of bad film is now the rage, I wish they'd revive this much-ignored great genre. *Isle of Levant, The Garden of Eden, Naked Island, Nature Camp Diary, Mr. Peek-A-Boo's Playmate*—all classics of a sort. Happy, healthy idiots on pogo sticks with air-brushed crotches was my idea of sexy. I've noticed a few shops in New York that seriously collect the magazines of this period, but not once have I seen a retrospective of nudist camp films anywhere in the world. Come on, Museum of Modern Art Film Department, stop snoozing on the job! It's your duty to preserve these embarrassing classics before the nitrate completely turns to ash.

In the eighties there's not much left of the burlesque circuit, but I still go occasionally. Scattered around the country, a few of the great houses are still alive, but barely; they stay open mainly as an excuse to show porn movies, and the strippers don't even bother to strip anymore. They come *out* nude, carrying a gym mat and a bottle of hand lotion, and get quite disgusting immediately. Sometimes it's so bad it's funny. A few years ago I went to one of the last remaining striptease shows in Baltimore, across the street from the long-defunct Gayety. It was about a hundred degrees inside. There were three other paying customers. The first stripper came out and she had tattoos, dirty bare feet, and a mild paunch. As she did her act, she completely ignored the audience and instead carried on a loud conversation with her girlfriend who was waiting for her in the back of the theater. "Hey, Crystal," she yelled in a thick Baltimore accent into the darkness. "We goin' over to Sylvia's? Get some beer!" "Yeah," hollered Crystal, "I got it. Hurry up. We're supposed to be there." "All right, already. I'm not off yet. I can't leave 'til ten," she growled back, all the while gyrating obscenely for the pitifully sparse audience. Finally through, she made a quick exit and was replaced by another "talent" I soon realized was dead drunk. She could barely walk, would stand there confused, mumbling incoherently, struggling to unbutton her outfit. Finally nude, she staggered precariously close to the edge of the stage and apparently got the whirlies. The two old men up front hastily retreated to the safety of the third or fourth row.

Suddenly, the manager stormed into the theater and started screaming, "Okay, Tammy, you're fired! I told you not to go on! Pack up and get out!" Tammy stood there confused, finally comprehended, gave him the finger and promptly fell off the stage, passed out cold. "Jesus Christ Almighty," yelled the manager as he rushed to the front of the theater and tried to drag out her dead weight. I joined the other few gentlemen who were running for the exits, but I have to admit in its own special way it was a show to rival my fondest days of Ol' Burlesque.

Down the street on Baltimore's "world famous" Block is the one last remaining "class" strip joint in town, the 2 O'Clock Club. Blaze sold it years ago, but the new owners try to keep the atmosphere alive. The first time I went back, I was thrilled to see that an old childhood friend from Lutherville, Maryland, was the headline stripper. What on earth did her parents think? I wondered. She took me backstage and proudly showed me all her expensive theatrical costumes and introduced me to the other girls, some of whom I soon realized used to be boys, or still were from the waist down. The tipsy businessmen in the audience had no idea that the "dates" for whom they bought drinks between routines and sometimes kissed might have once been named Leroy. One had an amazingly talented act: She began by lying prone on the floor, her ankles wrapped around a chair's legs. The drum rolled and, suddenly, she did a summersault in the air and somehow landed sitting in the chair stage center. Ta dum! Thunderous applause. I thought she was great but was even more impressed by Baby Buns, a three-hundred-pound comedienne, who actually picked up a barstool with her mammoth breasts and strutted around the stage. My friend the headliner was the last act and she was really good—professional, sexy, and, like the old days, proud to be a burlesque star. I wish she could travel with me and open my act in the colleges and cinema rep houses. We could really stir up some trouble.

For years, I traveled "promoting" my films which, in effect, means doing the lecture circuit for free. Sometimes I think the only reason I still try to get a movie together is because of the fringe benefits of free airline tickets. From Rio to Kent State, Ohio, I've gotten to see the world gratis. The only guest list that really matters is the airlines, especially if it's to Europe. I'm not the backpacking type, but if somebody's holding my hand, translating the language, paying for the meals, I'll talk about anything and answer the same old questions until the sound of my own voice ringing in my ears is pure torture. I never understand so-called celebrities who think it's beneath them to promote their work. Don't they want people to see it? Don't they realize that publicity is a free ad? It *is* called *show* business. Aren't they flattered somebody's interested?

I even went to Iceland for a week. The Reykjavík Film Festival. In the dead of winter, yet, when there's only a few hours of sunlight a day. "You're crazy," showbiz know-it-alls told me. "There's only a handful of movie theaters in the whole country. You can't make money there." But anywhere that both dogs and beer are illegal sounds OK to me. My hosts were charming, even the very proper lady from the festival who politely greeted me with, "I hear your films are just terrible." I never figured out if she was being brutally frank or if something was lost in the translation, but I thanked her just the same. That night for dinner the festival people decided to give me a little of my own medicine. We went to a fancy restaurant which specialized in traditional Icelandic food. The main course was a sheep's head and you were supposed to eat the eyeballs. Remembering my mother's advice to me as a child, "When in Rome do as the Romans," I tried not to react. They all waited with obvious glee as I followed their eating instructions. First you gouge out the eye socket and eat it, nibbling your way up to the big payoff—the eyeball itself. What the hell, I thought, as I tried to swallow the gristle. Here goes. I popped the eyeball into my mouth, bit down and felt an explosion similar to a cherry tomato. Beer may be illegal, but Brenavin, Iceland's delicious liqueur, is not, and I skipped dessert and had a few fast ones.

Sometimes invitations come from the strangest places. I was invited to a film festival in Milan partially sponsored by the Communist Party, which wanted to be connected to the youth vote at election time. Once I arrived, I quickly realized Italian Communists weren't the cliché kind—they didn't fall in love with their tractors or that sort of thing. They wore Armani suits, ate in fancy restaurants, and were incredibly generous hosts. We even got "food stamps" that were only accepted at one of Milan's snootiest and best restaurants. The only drawback was the "hotel" where Communists' guests were housed—nowhere near the "cell" I feared, but not exactly a rip-roaring night spot. The staff hated the American film directors; maybe we didn't look like the type who thought about "government" enough. I tried to be serious while waiting in the lobby between screenings, but every once in a while, I'd laugh maniacally and immediately feel guilty.

Months before Italy, I had cooperated with an Italian boyfriend of my sister's, who wanted to make a documentary about me. The main stars of the film are my parents. We had been told the film was being produced for Italian television only and would never be shown in America. Unfortunately, most of my films were banned in Italy so nobody there was much interested in a portrait of a film director whose films had never played in the country. So it opened in America instead. It's impossible to watch a documentary on yourself without feeling dead. I felt I was listening to my family and friends talk about me from inside my coffin. Once or twice my distributor booked it with one of my lectures in America, but it was too nerve-racking for me to be waiting backstage and hear my mother's voice booming out into an auditorium. I did think of a perfect way to promote it: In each city we could set up on stage an exact replica of my parents' dining room; Mom and Dad could travel with me and we'd reenact fights we've had over the years. They didn't even laugh when I mentioned the possibility.

I really felt like hot shit in Paris. Jean-Pierre Jackson, a Frenchman who knows bad taste when he sees it, had translated my first book, *Shock Value*, and it was being released in French as *Provocation*. He arranged a retrospective of my films at the Cinémathèque Française and was opening *Female Trouble* in his commercial movie house. I was thrilled to be spreading bad taste in a country known for its good taste. Imagine my disappointment when I showed up at my premiere to see a much bigger line *across* the street at another theater. "What's playing there?" I asked Jean-Pierre in a huff. "Loosely translated," he said, "the title would be *They Lick from Behind.*" Upstaged again.

Of course, nothing could top the very creative bum who waited outside my hotel at the Cannes Film Festival. As I exited, he shouted, "Monsieur Waters," stuck a needle through his neck, stretched out an upturned palm, and said, "Five francs, *si'l vous plaît.*" I was so appalled that I didn't give him any money, although, on hindsight, he deserved a lot more than he asked for.

Traveling in America, I always get to see the worst tourist sights and meet all the wrong people. And this time I was paid to "promote." When I hit the road with "An Evening with John Waters," my reputation preceded me, and all the wonderful lunatics who have supported my films for years would show up at the theaters and offer to take me to the local sights their respective Chambers of Commerce were trying to hide. In Atlanta, I was immediately whisked away to the street corner where Margaret Mitchell was run over by a taxicab. In Chicago, I discovered upon checking into the hotel that a fan had left me a hand-drawn detailed map to the one-time home of mass-murderer John Wayne Gacy. I suspected that it was the same little rascal who had mailed me a soil sample from Gacy's lawn, neatly labeled in a scientific specimen jar. I wanted to thank this mysterious fan since his gift had sat on my bookshelf for months, horrifying my visitors. It even spawned a whole Gacy collection I wasn't sure I wanted in the first place. One of my best friends in New York, who is also a little morbidly crazy, had written to Gacy on Death Row and commissioned an original oil painting by him of the witch in Disney's *Snow White*. I received it for Christmas. It was so creepy that even I had trouble hanging it and couldn't wait to tell my new Chicago friend about it. We went out after the show and had a lovely little drink together. It's on nights like those you thank the good Lord for being alive.

I was nervous about going to Portland because I was afraid it might be like being trapped with the "Secaucus Seven." Much to my relief, there wasn't a headband in sight and it turned out to be one of the best cities on the tour. I even had an opening act, but it wasn't the juggler or tumbler I had in mind. It was a drag queen. A perfectly nice one, but my audience is a little beyond that. Female impersonators seem so corny that I always feel like a Negro watching a minstrel show. I've never understood why *anybody* would want to imitate, much less be, Barbra Streisand, Carol Channing, or Diana Ross. Now if they did Janet Flanner, Pauline Kael, or even Mother Teresa, maybe I'd understand.

Probably the most bizarre invitation I received was to the White House. The Reagan White House. I was scheduled for my dog and pony show at the Biograph in D.C. and the week before got a call from one of the president's advisers on political affairs. He was a buff on exploitation pictures and invited me to lunch at the White House the day after my retrospective began. "Can I bring a date?" I asked, and he said "Yes, as long as the person can pass a security check." I brought a man, but he didn't seem to mind. I was amazed that *I* had passed the security clearance since I had visited one of the Manson Family in jail for years. Just how thorough *is* a security clearance, I wondered? Our host's office was the original one where the Watergate scandal was born. He showed us where the tape recorders were hidden and, best of all, the button next to Nixon's toilet labeled "Emergency." At first I was shocked to think that this was *the* button to start a nuclear war, but soon realized it was for a health emergency or, better yet, to summon a secretary if Nixon had a brilliant idea while on the can. We ate in the White House dining room for guests and talked about movies such as Chesty Morgan's *Deadly Weapons* (she kills people with her breasts), *The Undertaker and His Pals, Please Don't Eat My Mother,* and other cinematic shockers. The president's man was as well informed on these matters as he must have been on political affairs. We got the complete tour—Oval Office, Rose Garden—but I didn't get to see the Reagans' newly decorated screening room. The president was out of town but when Nancy was buzzed by a security guard, she said, "No, if you go in there we'll have to have a whole new security sweep after you leave." We were given sets of presidential seal cufflinks in a blue box decorated with Reagan's signature. I was most appreciative since without a souvenir nobody I know would have believed the whole day. Back on the street, dazed in the real world, I really felt patriotic for the first time. I wanted to wave the flag and sing "The Star Spangled Banner." Only in America could you get invited to a Republican White House for making films that the very administration would pay to have burned.

I was nervous only once. The Baltimore Museum of Art gave me a three-day retrospective of all my work with a black-tie opening. Talk about your own backyard! I followed a Grandma Moses exhibit. Somehow I was suddenly respectable. It was as if, magically, the film had changed content in the cans over the years. Here I was being honored for work I had feared being imprisoned for a decade before. My parents were in the opening night audience watching *Female Trouble* for the first time. I introduced them from the stage and was amazed to see my father signing an autograph later in the night. The mayor even proclaimed it "John Waters Day" in Baltimore. Could I have ordered all the beauty shops in town to give free bouffant hairdos for the day? I wondered. The only dissenting voice (in public at least) was from my old nemesis, Mary Avara, one-time head of the now-defunct Maryland Censor Board. "I can't believe a municipal museum would do something like this," she fumed to the Baltimore *News American*. "I don't want my tax money spent that way. I blame him for what's going on out there. Ladies can't walk the streets without some kid grabbing their purses. These kids would steal your garbage cans. The other day I found dead rats in my basement. People see his movies and get the know-how; they get the idea for all these rapes and hold-ups. To tell you the truth, I try not to even think of him. I wipe him from under my feet."

Just when you think everything is finally working out, something goes wrong. The very weekend of the museum retrospective I was forced to deal with a bust. *Pink Flamingos*, of course, was causing trouble once again after all these years. It seems there was a raid on a video shop in Phoenix, Arizona, and one of the porno tapes, *Inside Seka's Asshole* (or something similar), was nailed. At the trial, the defense lawyer for the porno told the judge, "You think *this* is bad, look at this one (*Pink Flamingos*), available in the very same shop." Wouldn't you know it, the porno got off and I got hassled. The judge moralized, "I can understand why some people in loneliness would rent porno, but why anybody would rent this one is beyond me." Suddenly, *Pink Flamingos* was heaty in the very respectable movie theater in Phoenix where it had played on and off for years. A reporter sent me a copy of the police report by the cop sent to the screening, written in his best *Dragnet* style. "The first scene opens showing a large w/f 'Edie' sitting in child's playpen wearing some type of underwear." He actually sat through the whole film and described it as if he were at a murder site or a car accident. It was the funniest review I ever read, but we had to sneak the print out of town before it was seized. So much for art. They were not impressed.

I get very strange mail. My favorite is from a kid named Freddy who wrote, "I'm in high school and I make films like you do. How come I get sent to the school psychiatrist and you get sent to Europe?" Another kid wrote volunteering to eat live rats on film. And probably the oddest was the guy who confessed, "My hobby is collecting sex with celebrities. I don't 'fuck and tell.' My other goals, besides you, are Pee-wee Herman, David Letterman, Grace Jones, Laurie Anderson, all the stars of *Rocky Horror*, and Klaus Nomi (so what if he's dead)." The only letter that really made me nervous was from a girl in Germany who wrote, "Your deathly face haunts me," and threatened, "One day I will show up on your doorstep." And she did. I didn't let her up, but agreed to meet her at the theater my friend Pat Moran runs because I knew Pat could intimidate a rattlesnake if she had to. The girl turned out to be harmless, but she still sends long, inappropriately intimate letters and presents which I always try to discourage. And candy. *Lots* of German chocolate that everybody tells me not to eat in case she's poisoned it. I always vow not to touch it and it sits there getting stale for months until, in a weak moment, I need a little midnight snack.

If you want your occupation to be "talking," it's fairly easy to get started. Conquer your fear of public speaking early. Just swallow your pride and start blabbing. Practice on family and friends first. Prepare a little talk on "Why You Are Getting on My Nerves" and surprise your parents by setting up a makeshift lectern immediately after supper. If you have brothers and sisters, form a debating team with them and challenge your parents on touchy subjects such as "Being Grounded Is Fascism" or "Curfew Violations Are a Birthright." Once you feel semiconfident, hit the streets. The age-old soapbox still works. Set one up at your high school and be sure to pick topics your audience will pay attention to—"Why Homework Is Unconstitutional" or "The History of Teacher Abuse in America in the Late 1970s." Always include a question-and-answer period, since all lazy public speakers know this pads the running time and gets the audience to do all the work. Argue a lot; practice makes perfect. Be opinionated on everything, since middle-of-the-roaders always end up in the audience, never on stage. Walk up to strangers and give them an impromptu lecture on "Happiness Is Being a Paranoid Schizophrenic." He or she will be so surprised they'll probably give you a quarter if you ask and, presto, you are no longer an amateur. You can start taking deductions off your income tax. Graduate to griping over any pet peeve at neighborhood improvement association meetings, become a self-appointed authority on anything, and start sending out flyers to special interest groups. By now you will probably have to get an agent—the pimps of ego, who certainly deserve their money since, after a point, it becomes embarrassing calling up prospective buyers and saying, "I have this really incredibly well-informed, funny speaker—ME." Once you get your mouth in the door, there's no one to tell you to shut up. You can harangue your way around the world, prattling and ranting to your heart's content.

Once you've become a pro, there's some practical advice I'd like to pass along. Never show up fifteen minutes before showtime. You will be treated to the sight of your sponsor nervously pacing up and down worrying about the box-office receipts and, if the take is a bit disappointing, you will see his charm melt right before your eyes. Nobody needs to hear "I was hoping for a sellout" right before you go on. Always be nice to everybody you meet. As soon as you leave town, word will begin spreading on the lecture circuit as to how difficult or cooperative you were. There's no better gossip than "What an asshole!" a certain celebrity was and word will catch up with you fast. I always ask in each city, "Who was the worst celebrity you ever booked?" and the stories are told with obvious relish. Always do talk shows. They treat you nicely (limo, nice hotel) and, in certain sections of the country, virtually define what is "hip" to your target audience. Avoid lecturing in discos; the audience is usually not in the mood but if you can stand it, the managements are all semi-legal and you always get paid in cash. Finally, never act like you're bored, even if you've heard the questions a million times. *These* people haven't asked it before. Put yourself on automatic pilot, think about your laundry, a book you're reading, anything. Always act like it's the first time you ever told a particular anecdote. Being on the lecture tour is a little like running for office. You must act popular even if you're secretly contemplating suicide. Living the life of a third-rate Mondale pounding the campaign trail is better than working, isn't it? Pull lever 6-C.

8

Why I Love the *National Enquirer*

The best thing about subscribing to the *National Enquirer* is that it arrives in the mailbox the same day as *The New York Review of Books*. How well rounded I feel. Happily snatching this national institution from the slot, I wonder if the mailman thinks I'm a slob for getting it. To hell with him, I figure, as I scan the headlines, hoping they'll top "Barry Manilow: I've Got a Big Nose—and I Like It!" Riding the elevator up to my apartment, I feel so lucky to be a subscriber. After all, the *Enquirer* boasts the largest circulation of any paper in the country, and it's one of the few chances I have to participate in something so genuinely mainstream. For once, I feel normal. Like millions of others, I, too, love the *National Enquirer.*

I'm secretly jealous of every celebrity hounded by this great tabloid, since only the really big stars need be worried. Coverage in the *National Enquirer* proves you're hot; it's the only true barometer of fame in America. Every day I feel depressed that no paparazzi jump out from behind a bush when I go across the street to get cigarettes. Being featured in the *Enquirer* has been a lifelong dream of mine; even a date with Suzanne Somers might be worth it.

Think how exciting it must be to have eight-hour shifts of reporters camped outside your building, hoping to get a shot of whomever you might be sleeping with. Or bartenders or waiters being bribed to reveal even the most mundane details of your life. Aren't stars impressed that *anyone*—much less 15 million readers—cares that they prefer a tuna sandwich to salami?

Does the *Enquirer* really hurt celebrities? I doubt it, not in the way *Confidential* did in the 1950s or even Louella Parsons or Hedda Hopper did before that. What the *Enquirer* does is *embarrass*, but at least it picks on the living and gives them a chance to fight back. Although some agents reportedly make deals to "lay off my clients" in return for dirt about others, nobody is really safe. Joan Rivers is always shouting, "Grow up, read the *Enquirer*," but the editors disregarded this apple polishing and published one of the most unflattering, horse-faced photos of her imaginable. Letting bygones be bygones, Liberace was smart enough not to hold a grudge in a no-win situation. He gave the *Enquirer* an interview even though it had supposedly ruined his career by publishing details from the "gayimony" lawsuit filed by his former bodyguard. Mr. Showmanship said the scandal actually brought him new fans.

I'm convinced that typical *Enquirer* readers move their lips while they read, are physically unattractive, badly dressed, lonely, and overweight. Especially overweight. Since the paper treats everyone except its readers badly, it's OK to be a behemoth as long as you're a nobody. Witness the "Fattest Couple" contests, in which roly-poly closet celebs compete for a measly $200 prize by sending hideous snapshots of themselves for publication. Or the endless pages of advertising for suspicious weight-loss schemes. But if you're fat *and* famous, beware; the *Enquirer*'s most vitriolic copy will be aimed your way. The first headline I clipped for my collection of fat exposés was "167 Pounds! That's a Lotta Liz." I guess the then-chubby Liz had hopped on the scale in some hotel suite and a telephoto lens zoomed in on the exact reading. Or what about wonderful Anita Ekberg, featured in "then and now" shots, naturally looking beautiful in her early career, but now hugely overweight, wrapped in a blanket, with no makeup, clutching a carrot from her garden in what she, mistakenly, assumed was the privacy of her own backyard. The headline read, "Anita Ekberg . . . What a Waist!" My all-time favorite, however, was "Whale of a Gal! That's Tubby Tina Onassis." Listen to the copy accompanying the eye-popping photos of Tina at the height of her career as the Fatty You Love to Hate Because She's So Rich. If there were a Pulitzer for trash, this writer would deserve the award: "Fat cat Christina Onassis is worth a ton of money, and she's turning into a whopper herself. Tubby Tina, dubbed 'Thunder Thighs' by the European press, is so fat she has to be helped out of her helicopter. The roly-poly 31-year-old heiress waddles away from her chopper—no doubt to get herself a square meal."

Even though the *Enquirer* no longer has staff photographers, it remains one of the top-paying purchasers of celebrity paparazzi shots. A front-page photo can fetch more than $2,000, and even "floaters" (pictures of cute animals, babies) can bring $400. No photo credit is ever given, but the money is so good, no one complains. "Ugly shots" are always welcome. Take the extremely unflattering photo of Robert Redford in the glare of the sun, with this screaming headline: "It Really IS Robert Redford." The caption read, "Redford's wrinkles are overcoming his dimples in this startlingly unretouched photo of the 47-year-old superstar, who's finally showing his age—and then some."

High fashion seems to be especially hated, by both editors and readers. The most outlandish outfits are featured with the prices prominently displayed and such copy as "So stiff and binding the model can't even sit down" or "This is going too far!" The skirts-for-men look is treated with terror. If one of the aliens the *Enquirer* so lovingly depicts ever were to read the paper, he'd assume that every man in America was contemplating whether to slip on a mini the next time he attended the Super Bowl. As much as high fashion is loathed, the paper's photo files of celebrities' outfits must be voluminous. Even Jackie herself might have laughed when they ran the headline "Oh No, Jackie O! She's Wearing the Same Outfit After 4 Years," with the pictures to prove it.

The *Enquirer*'s readers love death, and so do I. Who wouldn't buy its biggest-selling issue, the one with the photo of Elvis in his coffin on the cover? And how exciting to read about, and actually see, Michael Washington, a black man with his shirt open to the waist, who is now the proud owner of white hunk Jon-Erik Hexum's heart. Beating inside of him yet! And Baby Fae. God, what a controversy ("Baboon-Heart Baby Shocker"), what a *star*—just look at the innocent little darling. Look directly under that photo at the shot of the hideous baby baboon. How interesting to see the nice coverage her parents received in the *Enquirer* until they sold their exclusive story to *People* instead. Like a jilted lover, the editors responded: "Her Mother Is Wanted for Jumping Bail; Her Father Is a Drug Abuser Who Beat Her Mother." Bad taste has never been so naked. Or cheap. A mere 65¢ for all this? What a deal!

Being sick is also a big story. From nursing homes all over this great nation, shut-ins cry out for details. A gravely ill Peter Lawford or David Niven becomes a pinup for the terminally sick. Under oxygen tents, beside respirators, and in chemotherapy clinics, they want to know! Arthritis news is heralded almost weekly, even "2 Million Gout Sufferers" are not ignored. And the Betty Ford clinic; why, it must be the most glamorous place on earth! "Devastating Problems Have Taken Toll on Liza," shrieks the caption of a shocking photo taken before she checked in. And never fear, the *Enquirer* delivers what any self-respecting substance abuser wants to find out: "Treatment at Famed Drug & Alcohol Clinic Is a Living Nightmare—*Enquirer* Reporter Goes Undercover at Betty Ford Center." If only Liz Taylor had checked into *my* hospital, patients fantasize. Now that would be heaven on earth!

Even the lonely have a voice. My all-time favorite self-help piece in this civic-minded publication was "Want to Enrich Your Life? Just Go to a Coffee Shop—Here's How to Meet Interesting People." Its detailed plan for making new friends included: "(1) Always sit at the counter—never at a table. (2) Make sure that you're neatly dressed—people won't want to chat with a slob. (3) Strike up a conversation. Start by talking about the weather. (4) Greet the waitress with a smile . . . people would rather talk to someone who is smiling than to a grouch." The author of this profound advice, one Dr. Frank Caprio, warned, "Not all conversations over a cup of coffee will lead to something, but even if they don't, you can learn something that will enrich your life from everyone you meet." I wondered if the Dean sisters, two Baltimore spinsters whose sad lives were featured in the *Baltimore Sun*, had read this piece. Reportedly, they were so lonely that they kissed the furniture in their apartment, waved out their window to oncoming traffic, and hung out in doughnut shops saying hi to strangers until they got so desperate they held hands and jumped off a bridge together.

Sometimes the *Enquirer* tackles a real social issue: "Expert Claims Cabbage Patch Dolls Can Be Possessed by the Devil" was one howler scoop. The accompanying photo showed "famed psychic researcher Ed Warren" holding up a crucifix at a Cabbage Patch doll levitating over its crib. And you think these stories don't influence people? My cleaning lady, Rosa, who is so filled with great tales that Studs Terkel should marry her, recently confided her fear of Cabbage Patch dolls to me: "I heard about this woman who had one, and the doll tore up her china closet. The lady came downstairs, and her glasses were all broken. The dog started speaking in tongues and told her it was because she didn't wrap up the doll at Christmas."

"Oh, Rosa, you don't believe that," I said.

"Not really," she said, "but I'm leery of them. There's something about them, just like the devil. I don't want to be in the same room with a Cabbage Patch. My little grandson has one named Lester, and I tell him, 'Don't you be bringing Lester over here.' He just looks at me and laughs, but my son tells me, 'You're right, Mama, I don't like those dolls either.' "

After a top-selling issue treated the death of Grace Kelly with the same seriousness one would expect for the outbreak of nuclear war, the *Enquirer* began running updates on the attempt by a priest in Italy to have Grace canonized a saint. It was hinted that there were actual witnesses to miracles she had performed. I imagined Saint Grace at the premiere of *Rear Window*, stepping out of her limousine, the hem of her mink coat accidentally brushing across the face of a kneeling blind fan who is instantly cured of her affliction.

I also admire the *Enquirer's* gall when it ruins entire overhyped TV shows by revealing much-anticipated plot twists months in advance. Plots from *Dynasty* and the final episode of *M*A*S*H* were sneaked to the *Enquirer* by well-placed spies on the set and splashed across the front page. Being an espionage agent for the *Enquirer* is probably more lucrative than working for the Russians. Maybe the editors are doing a political service by keeping people in this line of work busy with ridiculous secrets that could hardly topple foreign governments. They're also keeping big-time do-gooders such as Billy Graham, Art Linkletter, and Lorne Greene out of trouble by publishing their folksy little advice columns on how to have happy little lives. The irony of these hypocrites' allowing themselves to be connected with the most despised scandal sheet in the professional Hollywood community, just because of its giant circulation, still amazes me. I must admit, however, that the New York subway-vigilante case was better handled by the *New York Post*. The *Enquirer* tried to convince you that the real-life Charles Bronson, Bernhard Goetz, had given them an exclusive interview, even though he refused. "Subway Vigilante—His Own Story," the headline screamed, despite the fact that the only sources in the article were police snitches. Two of his victims did take the bait, for a reported $300 each, but later bitched to *The Washington Post.* "The *Enquirer* robbed me," one said angrily. "My lawyer said I could have gotten at least $1,000."

I became sick of this whole story quickly. At first, the Archie Bunker outpouring of sympathy for Goetz got on my nerves, but then I started thinking, "Well, I don't blame him. I feel like shooting four or five people every time I step out of the house." Once, on a plane, I was deeply offended by a passenger seated near me who was guilty of the ultimate fashion violation—wearing summer white *after* Labor Day and before Memorial Day. Trying to be liberal, I hoped he was connecting later to some flight to the Caribbean, but his booming, drunken conversation soon convinced me this was not the case. Did he deserve to die for his hideous outfit? Would the readers of *Women's Wear Daily* and *GQ* have rallied wildly to my defense if I had blown him away?

When the parody the *Irrational Inquirer* was released in 1983, I was delighted at how funny it was. How difficult it must have been to parody a parody. Their joke headlines could almost have been the real thing: "I Died and Went to Heck"; " 'It's Hinckley's Baby,' Sobs Jodie"; "Dr. Tarnower's Diet Tips from Beyond the Grave."

But even more insane and ludicrous is the *Enquirer*'s bad stepchild, the one they never talk about, the rag put out apparently to utilize the old *Enquirer*'s black-and-white press—the *Weekly World News.* Closer in spirit to the old "I Ate My Baby" *Enquirer* before it got upscale enough to be sold in the supermarket, this fanatical, right-wing prime example of hepatitis-yellow journalism seems to be popular with illiterates and, not surprisingly, shock-loving hard-core punks and New Wavers. They even had Divine on the cover because irate viewers had complained to the BBC that she was "disgusting." The *News'* editorial policy can be best summed up by one of its stories: "Russkies Vow . . . We'd Blast Santa Out of Our Skies!" Whatever the rage in the other tabloids, they'll go further: "Ape Gives Birth to Human Baby" or "Vigilante Kills 27 Muggers." Sometimes their stories cheer me up considerably: "Good News for Smokers—It's Good for You."

Perhaps the most irresponsibly berserk columnist in the country, Ed Anger, is given space for his fanatical tirades each week in his column, "My America." He's beyond belief. His homophobia is legend—"Treat AIDS spreading sickos like the killers they are," he wrote once. "Is there any guarantee that the guy that used the water fountain in the park ahead of your little boy is not a gay with AIDS?" How about "Junk food made our country great: You never saw The Duke [John Wayne] strolling around munching a pita bread sandwich stuffed with alfalfa sprouts and sipping tea . . . If all Americans looked as washed out and wimpy as those broccoli Bruces, the Russkies would be dropping down on us and taking over right now." And best of all: "I'm madder than a doctor with a broken golf club at all this bellyaching about violence on TV when there's something even worse on the tube. I'm talking about the disgusting sex that's in most of today's top programs." Confirming everything I expected, an inside source of mine says Ed Anger is one Rafe Klinger, an "off-the-wall" guy who believes none of the stuff he cranks out.

The *News'* "TViews" column has such heads as "David

Letterman's Show Is Like Garbage—It Stinks." And their Ann Landers–type advice column, "Dear Dotti," can really dish out the hard-boiled advice—it's good to spank your children, and "the vast majority of kids between 13 and 18 are rotten—so rotten that their parents can barely tolerate them." But ultimately, the *Weekly World News* gets old quickly; its shock style becomes numbing, the celebrity gossip old hat and lifted from other papers I've already read, and I go back to the *Enquirer* for its, by comparison, class act.

Of course, the *Enquirer* isn't perfect. Its story format—with that opening punch—always promises more than it delivers, the "in mind" inner-thought quotes are pushed too far to be credible, and its self-congratulatory "You Read It Here First" pieces are a little pompous. The predictions every year leave me cold, and I'm sick of Princess Caroline—she's not even *American*, for God's sake. And the clip-out coupons to send to parole boards to demand that none of the Manson Family ever be released is my idea of a cheap shot.

But if only some of the more high-minded periodicals would follow the *Enquirer*'s example, maybe they'd pick up some much-needed circulation. Each publication has its own set of stars, and why are they immune? "Is Mr. Rogers' Marriage Falling Apart?" Readers of *Weekly Reader* would like to know. Wouldn't *The New York Review of Books* be a little spicier if they ran "Oriana Fallaci Is a Big Grouch" or "Isak Dinesen and Karen Carpenter—The Untold Link" or even "Gore Vidal Is Nellie." Couldn't the *Columbia Journalism Review* run stories such as "Helen Thomas Wears Same Outfit Every Day" or "Exclusive: Nora Ephron Nude!" What if the gay *Advocate* published "John Rechy Is Straight" or "Ronald Firbank Didn't Have to Die." And in the *National Review:* "Tricky Dicky and Rose Mary Woods—320 Whopping Pounds Together on the Scale." Or *Film Comment:* "Prediction: Jean-Luc Godard Will Remake *Ice Castles*."

Wouldn't this be fair game? If you don't want to be in the papers, be a plumber; I guarantee no one will be interested in your private life. But if you're in the public spotlight in any way, watch out!

"Does Nancy Kissinger Have Big Feet and Love It?"

"Has Jeane Kirkpatrick Ever Had Sex on a UFO?"

"Is Margaret Thatcher Having an Affair with Eddie Murphy?"

Who wants to know? *I* want to know.

9

"Ladies and Gentlemen . . .

the Nicest Kids in Town!"

If I have one regret in life, it's that I wasn't a Buddy Deaner. Sure, as a teenager I was a guest on this Baltimore show. I even won the twist contest with Mary Lou Raines (one of the queens of *The Buddy Deane Show*) at a local country club.

But I was never a Deaner. Not a real one. Not one of the Committee members, the ones chosen to be on the show every day—the Baltimore version of the Mouseketeers, "the nicest kids in town," as they were billed. The guys who wore sport coats with belts in the back from Lee's of Broadway (10 percent discount for Committee members), pegged pants, pointy-toe shoes with the great buckles on the side, and "drape" (greaser) haircuts that my parents would never allow. And the girl Deaners, God, "hair-hoppers" as we called them in my neighborhood, the ones with the Etta gowns, bouffant hairdos, and cha-cha heels. These were the first role models I knew. The first stars I could identify with. Arguably the first TV celebrities in Baltimore.

I'm still a fan—a Deaner groupie. I even named some of the characters in my films after them. So you can't imagine how excited I was when I finally got a chance to interview these local legends twenty years later.

The Buddy Deane Show was a teenage dance party, on the

air from 1957 to 1964. It was the top-rated local TV show in Baltimore and, for several years, the highest-rated local TV program in the country. While the rest of the nation grew up on Dick Clark's *American Bandstand* (which was not even shown here because Channel 13 already had *Buddy Deane*), Baltimoreans, true to form, had their own eccentric version. Every rock 'n' roll star of the day (except Elvis) came to town to lip-sync and plug their records on the show: Buddy Holly, Bill Haley, Fats Domino, the Supremes, the Marvelettes, Annette Funicello, Frankie Avalon, and Fabian, to name just a few.

You learned how to be a teenager from the show. Every day after school kids would run home, tune in, and dance with the bedpost or refrigerator door as they watched. If you couldn't do the Buddy Deane Jitterbug (always identifiable by the girl's ever-so-subtle dip of her head each time she was twirled around), you were a social outcast. And because a new dance was introduced practically every week, you had to watch every day to keep up. It was maddening: the Mashed Potato, the Stroll, the Pony, the Waddle, the Locomotion, the Bug, the Handjive, the New Continental, and, most important, the Madison, a complicated line dance that started here and later swept the country.

Although the show has been off the air for more than twenty years, a nearly fanatical cult of fans has managed to keep the memory alive. The producers of *Diner* wanted to include *Buddy Deane* footage in their film, but most of the shows were live and any tapes of this local period piece have been erased. Last spring five hundred people quickly snapped up the $23 tickets to the third Buddy Deane Reunion, held at a banquet hall in East Baltimore, to raise money for the Baltimore Burn Center. Buddy himself, the high priest, returned for the event. And more important, so did the Committee, still entering by a special door, still doing the dances from the period with utmost precision. I was totally star-struck and had as much fun that night as I did at the Cannes Film Festival. All on tacky Pulaski Highway.

In the beginning there was Arlene. Arlene Kozak, Buddy's assistant and den mother to the Committee. Now a receptionist living in suburbia with her husband and two grown children, Arlene remains fiercely loyal, organizing the reunions and keeping notebooks filled with the updated addresses, married names, and phone numbers of all "my kids."

She met Winston J. "Buddy" Deane in the fifties when she worked for a record wholesaler and he was the top-rated disc jockey on WITH—the only DJ in town who played rock 'n' roll for the kids. Joel Chaseman, also a DJ at WITH, became program manager of WJZ-TV when Westinghouse bought it in the mid-fifties. Chaseman had this idea for a dance party show, with Buddy as the disc jockey, and Buddy asked Arlene to go to work for him. On the air "*before* Dick Clark debuted," the show "was a hit from the beginning," says Arlene today.

The Committee, initially recruited from local teen centers, was to act as hosts and dance with the guests. To be selected you had to bring a "character reference" letter from your pastor, priest, or rabbi, qualify in a dance audition, and show in an interview ("the Spotlight") that you had "personality." At first the Committee had a revolving membership, with no one serving longer than three months.

But something unforeseen happened: The home audience soon grew attached to some of these kids. So the rules were bent a little; the "big" ones, the ones with the fan mail, were allowed to stay. And the whole concept of the Committee changed. The star system was born.

If you were a Buddy Deane Committee member, you were on TV six days a week for as many as three hours a day—enough media exposure to make Marshall McLuhan's head spin. The first big stars were Bobbi Burns and Freddy Oswinkle, according to Arlene, but "no matter how big anyone got, someone came along who was even bigger."

Joe Cash and Joan Teves became the show's first royalty. Joanie, whose mother "wanted me to be a child star," hit the show in early 1957 at age thirteen (you had to be fourteen to be eligible, but many lied about their ages to qualify), followed a few months later by Joe, seventeen. Like many couples, Joe and Joan met through the show and became "an item" for their fans. Many years later they married.

"I saw the show as a vehicle to make something of myself," remembers Joe. "I was aggressive. I wanted to get into the record business"—and years later he did.

Joe started working for Buddy as "teen assistant" and, along with Arlene, oversaw the Committee and enforced the strict rules. You received demerits for almost anything: Chewing gum. Eating the refreshments (Ameche's Powerhouses, the premiere teenage hangout's forerunner of the Big Mac), which were for guests *only*. Or dancing with other Committee members when you were supposed to be dancing with the guests (a very unpopular rule allowed this only every fourth dance). And if you dared to dance the obscene Bodie Green (the Dirty Boogie), you were immediately a goner.

"I got a little power-crazed," admits Joe. "I thought I was running the world, so they developed a Board, and the Committee began governing itself." Being elected to the Board became the ultimate status symbol. This Committee's committee, under the watchful eye of Arlene, chose new members, taught the dance steps, and enforced the demerit system, which could result in suspension or expulsion.

Another royal Deaner couple who met on the air and later married was Gene Snyder and Linda Warehime. They are still referred to, good-naturedly by some, as "the Ken and Barbie of the show." Gene, a member of "the *first* Committee, and I underline *first*," later became president of the Board. Linda reverently describes her Committee membership as "the best experience I ever had in my life." They later became members of the "Permanent Committee," the hall of fame that could come back to dance even after retiring. "That was our whole social life, being a Buddy Deaner," says Gene. "It was a family: Buddy was the father, Arlene was the mother."

Even today Gene and Linda are the quintessential Deaner couple, still socializing with many Committee members, very protective of the memory, and among the first to "lead a dance" at the emotion-packed reunions. "Once a Deaner, always a Deaner," as another so succinctly puts it.

The early "look" of the Committee was typically fifties. And although few will now admit to having been drapes, the hairstyles at first were DAs, Detroits, and Waterfalls for the guys, and ponytails and DAs for the girls, who wore full skirts with crinolines and three or four pairs of bobby socks. Joe remembers "a sport coat I bought for $5 from somebody who got it when he got out of prison. I was able after a while to afford some clothes from Lee's of Broadway" (whose selection of belted coats and pegged pants made it the Saks Fifth Avenue of Deaners).

One of the first ponytail princesses was "Peanuts" (Sharon Goldman, debuting at fourteen in 1958, Forest Park High School), who went on the show because Deaners were "folk heroes." She remembers Paul Anka singing "Put Your Head on My Shoulder" to her on camera as she did just that. She became so popular that she was written up in the nationwide *Sixteen* magazine.

"On the show you were either a drape or a square," explains Sharon. "I was a square. I guess Helen Crist was the first drapette: the DA, the ballet shoes, oogies [tulle scarves], eye shadow—eyeliner was *big* then—and pink lipstick."

Helen Crist. The best little jitterbugger in Baltimore. The first and maybe the biggest Buddy Deane queen of all. Debuting at a mere eleven years of age, taking three buses every day to get to the show, wearing that wonderful white DA (created by her hairdresser father), and causing the first real sensation. She was one of the chosen few who went to New York to learn how to demonstrate the Madison and was selected for the "exchange committee" that represented Baltimore's best on *American Bandstand*. She was the only one of the biggies who refused to be on the Board ("They had power; a lot were disliked because of it").

Helen's fans flocked to see her at the Buddy Deane Record Hops (Committee members had to make such personal appearances and sign autographs). "I got all these letters from the Naval Academy," Helen remembers, "so I went there one day, and all the midshipmen were hanging out the windows. It was a real kick!" Her fame even brought an offer to join the circus. "This man approached me, telegrammed me, showed up at the show. He wanted me to go to a summer training session to be a trapeze artist. I wanted to go, but my parents wouldn't let me. I was really mad. I wanted to join the circus."

Two other ponytail princesses who went on to the Buddy Deane hall of fame were Evanne Robinson, the Committee member on the show the longest, and Kathy Schmink. Today they seem opposites. Over lunch at the Thunderball Lounge, in East Baltimore, Kathy remembers, "I could never get used to signing autographs. 'Why?' I'd wonder." She wasn't even a fan of the show. "It was a fluke. My mother wanted me to go; she took me down to the tryouts. At first I was so shy I hid behind the Coke machines."

But Evanne "used to come right home and head for the

TV. I had always studied dance, and I wanted to go on [the show]. I'm the biggest ham." Although she denies being conscious of the camera, she admits, "I did try to dance up front. I wasn't going to go on and not be seen." But even Evanne turned bashful on one show, when Buddy made a surprise announcement. "I was voted prettiest girl by this whole army base. I was so embarrassed. Buddy called me up before the cameras, and I wasn't dressed my best. The whole day on the show was devoted to me."

Being a teenage star in Baltimore had its drawbacks. "It was difficult with your peers," recalls Peanuts. "You weren't one of them anymore." Outsiders envied the fame, especially if they lost their steadies to Deaners, and many were put off by boys who loved to dance. "Everybody wanted to kick a Buddy Deaner's ass," says Gene, recalling thugs waiting to jump Deaners outside the studio.

"It was so painful. It was horrible," says Joe. "I used to get death threats on the show. I'd get letters saying, 'If you show up at this particular hop, you're gonna get your face pushed in.' " And Evanne still shudders as she recalls, "Once I was in the cafeteria. One girl yelled 'Buddy Deaner' and then threw her plate at me. My mother used to pick me up after school to make sure nobody hassled me."

The adoring fans could also be a hassle. "I must have had ten different phone numbers," says Helen, "and somehow it would get out. There were a lot of obscene phone calls."

And the rumors, God, the rumors. "They all thought all the girls were pregnant by Buddy Deane," remember several. "Once I was off the show for a while, and they said I had joined the nunnery," says Helen, laughing. "It was even in the papers. It was hilarious."

Some of the rumors were fanned on purpose. Because *Buddy Deane*'s competition was soap operas, the budding teenage romances were sometimes played up for the camera. "One time I was going with this guy, and he was dancing with this guest I didn't like," says Evanne. "Buddy noticed my eyes staring and said, 'Do the same eyes.' And the camera got it." Kathy went even further. "I was with this guy named Jeff. We faked a feud. I took off my steady ring and threw it down. We got more mail: 'Oh, please don't break up!' Somebody even sent us a miniature pair of boxing gloves. Then we made up on camera."

Romance was one thing; sex was another. Most Deaner girls wouldn't even "tongue-kiss," claims Arlene, remembering the ruckus caused by a Catholic priest when the Committee modeled strapless Etta gowns on TV. From then on, all bare shoulders were covered with a piece of net.

Other vices were likewise eschewed. If a guy had one beer, it was a big deal. Some do remember a handful of kids getting high on cough medicine. "Yeah, it was Cosenel," says Joe. "They would drive me nuts when they'd come in the door, and I'd say, 'Man, you're gone. You are out of here. You are history.' "

Although many parents and WJZ insisted that Committee members had to keep up their grades to stay on the show, the reality could be quite different. With the show beginning at 2:30 in some years, cutting out of school early was common.

"I'd hook and have to dance in the back so the teachers couldn't see me," says Helen. "I *had* to get up there on time. My heart would have broken in two if I couldn't have gone on." Finally Helen quit Mergenthaler (Mervo) trade school, at the height of her fame. "The school tried to throw me out before. I couldn't be bothered with education. I wanted to *dance*."

"We had a saying: 'The show either makes you or breaks you,' " says Kathy. "Some kids on the show went a little nuts, with stars in their eyes; they thought they were going to go to Hollywood and be movie stars."

Yet Joe was a dropout when he went on the show and then, once famous, went *back* to finish. And according to Arlene, Buddy encouraged one popular Committee member (Buzzy Bennet) to teach himself to read so he could realize his dream of being a disc jockey. He eventually became one of the most respected programmers in the country and was even written up in *Time* magazine.

With the 1960s came a whole new set of stars, some with names that seemed like gimmicks, but weren't: Concetta Comi; the popular sister team of Yetta and Gretta Kotik. And then there was teased hair, replacing the fifties drape with a *Buddy Deane* look that so pervaded Baltimore culture (especially in East and South Baltimore) that its effect is still seen in certain neighborhoods.

Some of the old Committee kept up with the times and made the transition with ease. Kathy switched to a great beehive that resembled a trash can sitting on top of her head ("I looked like I was taking off"). And Helen, Linda, and Joanie all got out the rat-tail teasing combs.

Fran Nedeloff (debuting at fourteen in 1961, Mervo High School cha-cha) remembers the look: "Straight skirt to the knee, cardigan sweater buttoned up the back, cha-cha heels, lots of heavy black eyeliner, definitely Clearasil on the lips, white nail polish. We used to go stand in front of Read's Drugstore, and people would ask for our autograph."

Perhaps the highest bouffants of all belonged to the Committee member who was my personal favorite: Pixie (who died several years later from a drug overdose). "You could throw her down on the ground, and her hair would crack," recalls Gene. Pixie was barely five feet tall, but her hair sometimes added a good six to eight inches to her height.

But by far the most popular hairdo queen on *Buddy Deane* was a fourteen-year-old Pimlico Junior High School student named Mary Lou Raines. Mary Lou, the Annette Funicello of the show, was the talk of teenage Baltimore. Every week she had a different "do"—the Double Bubble, the Artichoke, the Airlift—each topped off by her special trademark, suggested by her mother, the bow. "We really sprayed it," remembers Mary Lou today from her home in Pennsylvania. "The more hair spray, the better. After you sprayed it, you'd get toilet paper and blot it. Sometimes you'd wrap your hair at night. If you leaned on one side, the next day you'd just pick it out" into shape.

Mary Lou was the last of the *Buddy Deane* superstars, true hair-hopper royalty, the ultimate Committee member. "We have a telegram," Buddy would shout almost daily, "for Mary Lou to lead a dance," and the cameraman seemed to love her. "When that little red light came on, so did my smile," she says, laughing. At her appearances at the record hops, "kids would actually scream when you'd get out of the car: 'There's Mary Lou! Oh, my God, it's Evanne!' Autograph books, cameras, this is what they lived for. They sent cakes on my birthday. They'd stand outside my home. They just wanted to know if you were real. I was honored, touched by it all."

Mary Lou was aware that in some neighborhoods it was *not* cool to be a Buddy Deaner. "Oh sure, if you were Joe College (pre-preppie), you just didn't do the *Deane Show*." "Did you ever turn into a Joe College?" I ask innocently. "No!" she answers, with a conviction that gives me the chills.

But as more and more kids (even *Deane* fans) *did* turn Joe College, many of the Committee made the mistake of not keeping up with the times. Marie Fischer was the first "Joe" to become a Committee member—chosen simply because she was such a good dancer. As with the drapes and squares of the previous decade, she explains, "there were two classes of people then—Deaners and Joe College. The main thing was your hair was *flat*, the antithesis of *Buddy Deane*," she says, chuckling. "I was a misfit. Every day I'd come to the studio in knee-highs, and I'd have to take them off. You *had* to wear nylons. Before long I started getting lots of fan mail: 'I think you're neat. I'm Joe, too.' There was a change in the works."

Part of that change was the racial integration movement. "I had a lot of black friends at the time, so for me this was an awkward thing," says Marie. "To this day, I'm reluctant to tell some of my black friends I was on *Buddy Deane* because they look at it as a terrible time."

Integration ended *The Buddy Deane Show*. When the subject comes up today, most loyalists want to go off the record. But it went something like this: *Buddy Deane* was an exclusively white show. Once a month the show was all black; there was no black Committee. So the NAACP targeted the show for protests. Ironically, *The Buddy Deane Show* introduced black music and artists into the lives of white Baltimore teenagers, many of whom learned to dance from black friends and listened to black radio. Buddy offered to have three or even four days a week all black, but that wasn't it. The protesters wanted the races to mix.

At frantic meetings of the Committee, many said, "My parents simply won't let me come if it's integrated," and WJZ realized it just couldn't be done. "It was the times," most remember. "This town just wasn't ready for that." There were threats and bomb scares; integrationists smuggled whites into the all-black shows to dance cheek-to-cheek on camera with blacks, and that was it. *The Buddy Deane Show* was over. Buddy wanted it to end happily, but WJZ angered Deaners when it tried to blame the ratings.

On the last day of the show, January 4, 1964, all the most popular Committee members through the years came back for one last appearance. "I remember it well," recalls Evanne.

"Buddy said to me, 'Well, here's my little girl who's been with me the longest.' I hardly ever cried, but I just broke down on camera. I didn't mean to, because I *never* would have messed up the makeup."

In 1985 the Committee members are for the most part happy and healthy, living in Baltimore, and still recognized on the street. "They kept their figures, look nice, and are very kind people," says Marie from her lovely country home before taking off for the University of Maryland, where she attends law school.

Most are happily married with kids and maintain the same images they had on the show. "We are kind of like Ozzie and Harriet," says Gene Snyder as Linda nods in agreement. "I'm a typical middle-class housewife," says Peanuts, "Girl Scout leader, very active in my kid's school." Mary Lou is still a star. That she has an affluent life-style surprises no one on the Committee. In her home, near Allentown, Pennsylvania, she serves me a beautiful brunch, models her fur coats, and poses with her Mercedes. "When I get depressed, I don't go to the psychiatrist; I go to the jeweler," she says.

Oddly enough, few of the Deaners I've talked to went on to showbiz. Joe Cash has Jonas Cash Promotions ("my own promotional firm—we represent Warner Brothers, Columbia, Motown—eighty-five percent of the music you hear in this market")—and Active Industry Research (a "research firm—I'm chairman of the board"). Evanne and her brother run the John Brock Benson Dance Studios and have a line of dancers who appear at clubs all over the state. But most have settled down to a *very* straight life.

And none are bitter. Although the Committee was a valuable promotional tool for WJZ at the time, and belonging was a full-time job, no one (except teen assistants) was paid a penny. Even doing commercials was expected. Mary Lou laughs at the memory of doing a pimple medicine spot on camera. And who can forget those great ads for the plastic furniture slipcovers that opened with the kids jumping up and down on the sofa and a local announcer screaming, "Hey, kids! *Get off that furniture!*"? Or the Bob-a-Loop? Or Harford Motor Coach Company? Or Snuggle Dolls? The Deaners didn't mind. As Marie puts it, "The rewards were so great emotionally that you didn't have to ask for a monetary award."

Many had difficulties dealing with the void when the show went off the air. Gene calls it "a big loss." "It was living in a fantasy world," says Helen, "and later on, growing up, it was a definite blow: reality." "I still have a whole box of fan mail," says Evanne. "If I'm ever depressed, sometimes I think, 'Well, this will make me feel better,' and I go down and dig in the box."

Holding on to the memories more than anyone is Arlene Kozak, who is by far the most loved by all the Committee members. (They gave her a diamond watch at the last reunion.) "Do you miss showbiz?" I ask her. "Not showbiz," Arlene answers, hesitating, "but the record biz, the people. Yes, I miss it very much. I don't think I'll ever get over missing it, if you want to know the truth."

Many of the Committee members' spouses faced an even bigger adjustment. In "mixed marriages" (with non-Deaners), many of the outsiders resented their spouses' pasts. "At twenty-one I married a professional football player," Helen remembers, "and he made me burn all the fan mail. I had trunks of it. He was mad because I was as popular as he was. He just didn't understand."

But some have dealt with the problems in good humor. When Mary Lou's husband gave me the long and complicated directions to their home on the phone, he ended with, "And there you will find, yes, Mary Lou Raines." He later confided that when he first started dating her, he had no idea of her early career. "Everywhere we went, people would say 'There's Mary Lou.' I wondered if she had just been released from the penitentiary."

The *Buddy Deane* phenomenon is hardly dead. Each reunion (and a new one is in the works) seems bigger than the last. Deaners seem to come out of the woodwork, drawn by the memory of their stardom. Buddy returns on a pilgrimage from St. Charles, Arkansas, where he owns a hunting and fishing lodge and sometimes appears on TV, to spin the hits and announce multiplication dances, ladies' choice, or even, after a few drinks, the Limbo. Some of the really dedicated Committee members get tears in their eyes. Was it really twenty years ago? Could it be?

Why not do the *Deane Show* on Baltimore TV again? Just once. A special. The ultimate reunion. From all over the country, the Deaners could rise again, congregate at the bottom of Television Hill, and start Madison-ing their way ("You're looking good. A big strong line!") up the hill to that famous dance party set, the one that now houses a talk show. The "big garage-type door" they remember would open, and they'd all pile in, past George and "Mom," the Pinkerton guards who used to keep attendance, and crowd into Arlene's office to comb their hair, confide their problems, and touch up their makeup. Buddy could take his seat beneath his famous Top 20 Board, and the tension would build. "Ten seconds to airtime.... three, two, one. *Ladies and gentlemen ... the nicest kids in town!*"

10

How to Become Famous

If you think about it, getting famous is easier than getting a job. And face facts, everybody wants to be famous. More than rich, more than happy, more than successful. So what are you waiting for? Quit school, forget that boring job, dismiss those nagging parents. Throw caution to the wind, get out your dark glasses, and prepare to blast off into the wonderful world of show business. Wouldn't you rather sign an autograph than kiss a girl? Have paparazzi annoy you and your star-struck bimbo date rather than enter a mature, predictable relationship that only ends in divorce? Be an asshole instead of a role model?

You know you're great, so why not be arrogant about it? Prove to your stupid little friends what they've been so blind about all these years. I'm not talking talent here—those condescending bastards are so stuffy, anyway—I'm talking celebrity: hype, openings, Liz Smith, the *New York Post*'s "Page 6," *People* magazine, the stuff that counts. Something that can give you what you really want in life: free drugs, groupies, star demands, and the delirious excitement of firing all the people who helped you claw your way to the top.

Take about five seconds and pick a career. Are you loud and ugly? Do you show an appalling lack of taste in clothes? If so, choose rock star. Were you good at cheating in math class? A film producer for sure. Did you just love it when you spread gonorrhea to half the sophomore class? The vocation of movie star is all yours. Did it say, "notorious liar" under your high-school yearbook picture? You, too, can be president. And if you always thrilled the gang spinning smutty little fibs about your sexual conquests, the best-seller list is your natural home.

Now that you've wasted your self-styled valuable time over this unimportant decision, let's move on to the serious stuff. How do you get famous? How do you make all those doubting fools of your boring past eat crow pie and beg to spend just one second in your golden company? Well, here goes: How to Become Famous in Ten Easy Steps.

1) **Exaggerate yourself.** It's much easier to get a reaction from the public. If you are overweight, go eat ten pies. If you are sickly and would get sand kicked in your face on any beach, start taking diet pills. Complexion problem? No big deal—rub a bag of potato chips on your face and change your name to "Pimples." Nothing matters as long as you have too much or too little of something. Anything.

Got a rotten disposition? Well, get meaner. Ryan O'Neal is not famous for his films so much as he is for punching out his son's two front teeth and being an all-around sourpuss. If you're an aspiring politician, make racist comments the press can overhear; the outrage may lose you your first election but it will get you lots of ink and make you a household word, and then you can make a successful "comeback" in the near future.

Change your name and kill off the old self who was just an average nobody. Would Merle Johnson (Troy Donahue) or Herbert Khaury (Tiny Tim) ever have made it with those embarrassing monikers? Aren't Halston and Meat Loaf really in the same boat? Think of that obscene stage name, Peter O'Toole. What could be filthier, Muff

O'Clit? Whatever your image in your old life, change it without warning, do the opposite of what people expect. If you're the high-school football star, throw out your jock and make a rock debut dressed in nothing but a woman's girdle and underarm perspiration shields. If you were the class nell, beaten up by the guys for risking expulsion rather than attending gym class, get back at those creeps by writing a scientific article about the high rate of impotency among high-school athletes. If you were the girl with the flattest chest and the ugliest face, shock your entire class by starring in a porno movie that gets busted at its campus premiere. If you had the lowest grade average in your class and were nicknamed "Knucklehead," plagiarize an out-of-print potboiler, publish it as your own, get caught, and hype your next book at the trial. In other words, get them talking, even if it's all negative word of mouth. What do you care as long as they spell your name right?

2) **Hype yourself.** Jayne Mansfield, the definitive movie star of all time, used to walk up Hollywood Boulevard early in her career, scantily clad in a leopard-skin bikini handing out autographed pictures of herself to confused passersby. When she decided to marry muscleman Mickey Hargitay in a glass see-through chapel, she promised the minister it would be a private ceremony. Realizing the stupidity of this vow, at the last minute she had hundreds of pink cards printed up and dropped from a helicopter over Hollywood that read "See Jayne Mansfield Married Under Glass," and went on to give the date, time, and location. Naturally, hordes of publicity gawkers trampled the grounds, ripping up flowers and turning the entire blessed event into chaos—and ensuring Jayne the front-page coverage for which she lived and died.

Follow the example of this great star and plot your

own campaign to fame. Do *anything* to get in the papers. Appear nude at the local elementary-school Maypole Queen celebration. Run from lawn to lawn in your neighborhood inserting shocking photos of yourself in everyone's Sunday paper. Mix some broken glass into your dinner at a fancy restaurant, cause a scene, sue, and magnanimously drop the charges, declaring that your damaged vocal cords have miraculously produced an exciting new singing voice. Make up fake investigative-journalism pieces, get caught, and get your paper in lots of trouble. Turn in your friendly boss, the only one who would hire you with your blue Mohawk, for minor health-code violations on the job and start a career as a consumer advocate. The next time *The Burning Bed* is rerun on TV, send out press releases to local news teams and let them know the exact time you plan on beating your wife. Accuse your high-school principal of child abuse and tour the talk shows as a spokesperson for abused teens. Go on, do *something*, for God's sake, or nobody will *ever* know you!

3) **Use your family.** Charity begins at home, they say, and many a showbiz career has been backed by rich relatives. If you're lucky enough to have rich parents, all the better. Determine their assets early in life so that when it's time for them to liquidate everything they own in order to finance your career, there won't be any confusion. If whining, screaming, and kicking your feet doesn't work, try using guilt as a tool of persuasion, and don't hesitate to throw up any real or imagined childhood unhappiness you may have experienced. If all else fails, blackmail them. Tell them that unless they cough up the bucks, you plan to get a sex change and move next door.

Once they agree, it helps to lie. If you want to make a low-budget horror shocker entitled *Suck My Guts*, don't tell them. Instead, make up a fake project to fit your parents' ideology. If Mom and Pop are liberals, pretend you want to make a PBS documentary spotlighting the health hazards of breakfast cereal for children. If conservative, how about a catchy title like *Bomb Biafra?* When they show up at the premiere, realize they've been had, and flip out, take their photo. It will help in future promotion of your product. What can they do about it anyway? Take away your allowance?

4) **Move to Europe.** Here you can lie all you want about your past accomplishments and not waste time by having to really *do* anything in America. Nobody will find out. Make up a wildly successful résumé and don't hold back on the fabrication. Tell them you had a Broadway hit that ran three years or the number-six record in Chicago. How will they know? Who are they going to call?

If you don't stay in one country too long and keep on moving, you can really get creative. Put together a scrapbook on your favorite star, superimpose your head on the photos, and actually take on the identity. Claim to *be* one of the original Shirelles or Vandellas and get bookings. Or comb the showbiz obits and take on the career of Edie Sedgwick or Patsy Cline and live their lives in Europe the way you think they *should* have lived. By the time anyone is wiser, you'll be back in America, rich, ready, and full of hype about your European success. Publicity breeds publicity, so you're on your way to the top in the only country that counts: America.

5) **Be an animal.** I know this sounds ridiculous, but think about it. Sometimes it's wiser to compete in a field where there's less competition. I mean, besides the has-beens (Lassie, Rin Tin Tin), the classics (Francis the Talking Mule, Mr. Ed), the contemporaries (Benji, Willard and Ben), and that brash newcomer Phar Lap the horse (who seems to be a phar-*lop* at the box office), who is there? If

you are an animal you can get loads of commercials, appeal to senior citizens as well as to kids, and, most important, have a chance to win the most coveted, prestigious Hollywood trophy there is, the Patsy Award—the animal Oscar, as it is known. Alvin, are you listening? Alvin! ALVIN!!!!

If you've been paying attention, you have learned how to at least get your foot in the door, so now I'd like to move on to Phase Two—How to *Remain* Famous. Sometimes this is a little trickier, but who wants to be a mere flash in the pan? Drastic steps have to be considered, so bear with me. Fame maintenance is even more important in making a lasting impression on all your envious friends from your past. Refuse to speak to them. Turn up your nose and prepare to snub. There'll be no talk of a "comeback" for you, thank you—you will *always* be a star.

6) **Have sexual problems.** And make them original. Better yet, hate sex and pontificate about what an embarrassing, messy activity it is and how humiliating the entire experience can be. If you are unlucky enough to be heterosexual and persist in having affairs anyway, make sure they are with a blood relation, preferably your mother or father.

   If you must write a kiss-and-tell autobiography, make sure your sexual trysts are at least original; your "wild night" with Don Knotts, the "heaven" of performing fellatio on Spiro Agnew, or the "nirvana" of satisfying Clara "Where's the Beef?" Peller orally. Try to boast of celebrities you've *never* had sex with (hopefully Shelley Winters, Alana Stewart, Maggie Trudeau), and if you insist on panting, make sure it's *truly* perverse (Yoko Ono, Henry Kissinger, Ed McMahon). Always remember that a mature, loving, normal relationship is sure career-icide. Avoid it at all costs.

7) **Get sick.** Immediately check into the Betty Ford Clinic but, instead of emerging victorious, drop out and start shooting heroin in your eyeballs on the set of your up-and-coming TV series. Give press conferences about other patients—how Mary Tyler Moore got you to try huffing glue or Liz Taylor snorting typewriter Wite-Out. Bitch about that real-life Nurse Ratched, Betty Ford herself, giving enemas, patrolling the halls, and smacking around celebrities who are going through "cold turkey."

Better yet, stop eating and claim you have anorexia, the trendiest, most envied disease of the day. Show up on *Johnny Carson* weighing sixty-seven pounds and plug your new diet book. Try jungle rot, beriberi, or leprosy—all original in 1986.

8) **Be unhappy.** The public likes nothing better than misery at the top. Drug addiction and public drunkenness are too commonplace to have much effect, but suicide attempts are always good for a bulletin. Try jumping off a building and *landing* on someone famous. Or stabbing yourself to death with a tiny safety pin. If your parents are famous, hope they are assassinated so you can get yourself prime-time TV funeral coverage. Always carry glycerine and an eyedropper with you in case the tear ducts dry up when they go in for a close-up.

9) **Kill somebody.** And make the victim famous—the only surefire route to overnight front-page fame. None of this buried gossip-column crap, either. Page one. Hard news. The Big Time. We're talking household word.

Start by stalking your favorite star. Pick one. Anybody. How about Katharine Hepburn? So snotty, so moral, so goddamn proper. Since we know Miss Hepburn goes bananas if any member of the audience *dares* to snap a photo of her on the Broadway stage, try strobing her with a flash camera in the middle of her next drama, screeching, "Go, Katharine, go! That's it! Give me some anger! Great, baby, great!" Watch her have a heart attack. You paid for your ticket, didn't you? What do they expect?

Rent a creepy little room somewhere and leave lots of cryptic notes around for the press to discover right after you strike. Better yet, a diary. Brood. Become obsessed. Never shave. Fantasize about what a relief jail will be—no phones ringing, free rent, a chance to finally work on your novel. And just think, maybe you'll get the electric chair and get on *60 Minutes*. If not, just savor the anticipation of being released. Finally you'll get some respect. When Charles Manson is eventually paroled, will *he* have to wait in line outside some crummy, trendy New York nightclub? The one that wouldn't let *you* in last week? Ha! Are you kidding? Right this way, Mr. Manson. Free drink tickets? You'd like to hear "Helter Skelter"? Yesssir!!

10) **Die.** Get murdered yourself. Drastic? Well, I thought you were serious. Isn't Sharon Tate more famous for being murdered than she is for any of her films? Didn't the careers of Indira Gandhi, Sadat, JFK, RFK all pick up and *last* after their splashy exits? Even the proper natural death can elevate you to the Hall of Fame—Henry Fonda took weeks and weeks of newsprint to finally die of old age.

Make sure you plan your funeral in advance so you can go in the style you want. Poor Jayne Mansfield didn't make her own arrangements and they buried her in Pen Argyl, Pennsylvania, for chrissake. Her own one-time press agent admits that Jayne would have wanted "a royal Hollywood funeral, to be surrounded by two dozen long-haired Italian boys in tight pants, with Chubby

Checker doing the Twist on top of her pink casket."
Plan ahead, Jayne. Plan ahead.

It also helps to have led a thoroughly despicable life,
so family and friends don't hesitate to spill all the beans
to venomous biographers who will ensure your notoriety
for the next few generations of celebrity watchers.

So you see, it's quite simple. Just follow these ten easy
steps and you, too, can be famous. After all, wouldn't you
rather be dead than unknown?

11

Guilty Pleasures

Being a Catholic, guilt comes naturally. Except mine is reversed. I blab on ad nauseam about how much I love films like *Dr. Butcher, M.D.* or *My Friends Need Killing*, but what really shames me is that I'm also secretly a fan of what is unfortunately known as the "art film." Before writing this sentence, I've tried to never utter the word "art" unless referring to Mr. Linkletter. But underneath all my posing as a trash film enthusiast, a little-known fact is that I actually sneak off in disguise (and hope to God I'm not recognized) to arty films in the same way businessmen rush in to see *Pussy Talk* on their lunch hour. I'm really embarrassed.

Give me black and white, subtitles, and a tiny budget, and I'm impressed. I really like snotty, elitist theaters in New York like Cinema III (my favorite because it's so comfortable and the ticket price is always expensive), or the Paris, where if you ask for popcorn they look at you as if you're a leper asking for heroin and sneer, "Really! We don't *have* refreshments." I'm so used to audiences yelling back to the screen in grind houses that it's a real break to sit with a well-behaved audience. I never eavesdrop in these theaters because the conversations are generally maddeningly pretentious. It's also a problem to laugh out loud at something only you may find funny (especially if it's a German film—Germany is not *ever* funny to these audiences). These cinema buffs are very touchy about humor and will turn around and scowl right in your face if they think your laugh is inappropriate.

Like every good film snob, I'm appalled if the films have been dubbed. Even though I can only speak English, dialogue in a foreign language always sounds more important to me. I pretend that somehow seeing those films will teach me a new language, but I guess I'll have to be truthful and admit that the only foreign expression I've mastered in twenty years of watching foreign films is *Das Boot*. So much for internationalism.

The one thing I do hate about arty theaters is the trailers which never feature the best scenes but concentrate on highbrow quotes such as "A masterpiece of cinema—Archer Winsten, *New York Post*" or "I'm in love with Laura Antonelli—Rex Reed, New York *Daily News*." Even the deadly serious cinephiles get a howl out of this, and I think arty coming attractions actually lose ticket buyers in the long run. What's the matter with a little hype in these situations? Wouldn't it interest moviegoers more to stick to the tried-and-true formula here? How about "See Bibi Andersson slit her wrists!" or "Watch as Bresson directs an entire film where nothing happens" or "At last! A film that is black and white, four hours long, and with subtitles—*The Mother and the Whore*—coming soon to a theater near you!"

As a Baltimore teenager, my filmgoing habits were completely schizophrenic. I'd see four films in one day—maybe start off with *Door to Door Maniac* starring Johnny Cash, and then rush to the opening-day matinee of *The Exterminating Angel*. After gobbling down a sandwich, I'd catch an evening screening of *Hagbard and Signe* at the most obscurely interesting art theater in town, the now-defunct 7-East, and then top it off with a late-night showing of something like *Angel, Angel, Down We Go*.

Since my influences were so confusing, I ended up making

lowbrow movies for highbrow theaters, but I only owned up to the trashy ones as a contributing factor. I guess it is time to come out of the art closet and admit that the following ten films influenced me as much as all the garbage I've so lovingly consumed in theaters all my life. It's like going to cinema confession and I'm sure my penance would be to make a good act of contrition and see *Ilsa, She Wolf of the SS* ten times. Only I wouldn't be heartily sorry, just eternally ashamed.

Interiors (1978, Woody Allen). Yes, *Interiors*. I know readers will think I'm being purposely perverse, but I think this film is a masterpiece, even though my face turns scarlet as I write. I even went back to see it for a second time last week because I didn't trust my initial rave reactions, but now I know I'm right. You name it, *Interiors* has it—anguish, divorce, suicide attempts, religion, sibling rivalry, inability to communicate—all my favorite topics for a "serious" film.

The performances are brilliant. Especially Geraldine Page. Just watching her facial expression as she's internally torn apart is alone worth the price of admission. No wonder she's crazy, with screen children that intensely pretentious. Two favorite scenes: E. G. Marshall telling Geraldine Page in church that he wants to remarry as she loses control, knocks over religious candles, and storms out of the church in a tracking shot that really rips you apart; and the suicide attempt scene that begins with close-ups of black masking tape angrily being ripped off the roll with ear splitting sound to seal up every window and door before turning on the gas. Even Bergman would be jealous.

Woody Allen should always direct serious films and never star himself in his own productions. If *Interiors* was filmed in Swedish with subtitles and directed under a *nom de plume*, it would have received the rave reviews it deserved, but instead critics seemed scandalized that Woody Allen didn't try to be funny and ended up treating it as if Russ Meyer had starred Twiggy in a film instead of one of his buxom beauties.

The Films of Marguerite Duras. Miss Duras makes the kind of films that get you punched in the mouth for recommending them to even your closest friends. If there is such as thing as *good* avant garde cinema, this is it. Even though I believe pretension is the ultimate sin, Marguerite Duras has taken pretension one level ahead of itself and turned it into a style. She is the ultimate eccentric. Her films are maddeningly boring but really quite beautiful. After seeing her work, I think I know what it must feel like to be hypnotized.

Perhaps her most impossible opus to date is *The Truck*. The entire film consists of the director sitting in a nondescript room with Gérard Depardieu as they read the script of the film while every ten minutes or so the monotony is replaced by yet another monotonous shot of a blue truck, endlessly but serenely driving through the French countryside. If Warhol did it for the Empire State Building, why can't Marguerite Duras do it for French trucks? All I know is that on my first trip to Cannes, in the cab from the Nice airport, I saw Marguerite's "trucks" a hundred times on the highway and felt hypnotized all over again. That's more than I can say for *The Car* or *Car Wash*.

Even better than seeing *The Truck* was seeing Marguerite Duras in person at the Carnegie Hall Cinema with the premiere of *India Song*. As I waited in line, the management saw me, started laughing, and let me in for free. The film is nearly perfect, if perfection is accomplishing what you set out to do no matter how absurd or affected the goal is. The film is so posed, so formal, and so glamorous that it almost isn't a movie at all—it's like watching a chic performance piece.

Afterward, Miss Duras begrudgingly appeared to "discuss" the film. She was better than my wildest dreams could imagine. To start off she refused to speak English and had a translator who couldn't or, as I suspected, wouldn't either unless the audience started yelling. The few comments I did manage to get were hysterical: "I don't really care if anyone sees my films," "I have made two new films but haven't decided if I will ever let anybody see them," and my favorite, "The way I prefer audiences to see my work is all the films one after another because it would be more difficult." I want to meet the people who give her the money to make these fabulous movies. They must be very, very rich or very, very insane.

Brink of Life (1958, Ingmar Bergman). In high school I used to sneak to a local college for a complete retrospective of the films of Ingmar Bergman. Except for *Scenes from a Marriage*, I still love Bergman (even *The Serpent's Egg*). But *Brink of Life* is my personal favorite. Three pregnant women locked in a maternity ward going through all sorts of agony over miscarriage, abortion, sexual frigidity, fear, unwanted children, and all other neuroses that seem to be to Sweden what tulips are to Holland. Revival houses almost never dig this one out of the vaults, and I wish they would. Come on, Ingmar, how about *Brink of Life II?*

Night Games (1966, Mai Zetterling). A real shocker when it was first released, *Night Games* was my all-time favorite film for many years. It so offended juror Shirley Temple Black that she quit the San Francisco Film Festival when the programmers refused to remove it from the schedule. Zetterling directs with a ludicrously melodramatic, overly gothic sledgehammer to deal with this story of impotence, child masturbation, cross-dressing, porno flicks, and vomiting.

Favorite scene: Ingrid Thulin giving birth to a dead child in the middle of a degenerate party as someone reads aloud "The Birth of Christ." Students of Regurgitation Throughout Cinema should note this was one of the first Swedish films to feature incredibly realistic vomiting. Another real master-piece that for some reason is almost never revived, along with her other two great films, *Loving Couples* and *Doctor Glas*. I hear Mai Zetterling is now in England directing a new feature. I can't wait to see it. With technology advances, just think what her vomiting scenes would be like today!

Teorema (1968). Pier Paolo Pasolini's most erotically Catholic film. God visits a bourgeois Italian family in the form of Terence Stamp, who never looked better before or after this role. Incidentally, Stamp's portrayal of God featured the first glimpses of frontal male nudity shown in international cinema and caused quite a storm. After seducing the entire family—businessman father, glamorous mother, frumpy daughter, nervous son (in baggy jockey shorts), and pious female servant—God vanishes and the whole family goes nuts. Father gives away his factory and strips naked in public, Mother picks up and seduces rough trade in her automobile. But the best is the finale, where the spookily religious servant levitates and then holy water gushes from her grave.

Salò (1975). Pasolini's last film before his rather legendary, if not Hollywood Babylon-y, death. *Salò* is a film people wouldn't expect me to feel guilty about liking. After all, it features shit eating, eyeball gouging, scalping, and female imper-sonations—subjects I've used in my own films and enjoyed in others: in short, the staples of modern entertainment. But I think *Salò* is anything but exploitation. Gulp, here's that word again, rearing its ugly head—ART.

Salò is a beautiful film with a very moral message: There is such a thing as being too powerful or too kinky, and it can produce nothing but despair. Italian youth (many with pim-ples—Pasolini's favorite) are kidnapped, tortured, humili-ated, sexually abused, and finally murdered by a group of Fascists. It's a harrowing film that features the most incredibly handsome sets and some of the best sound effects in screen history, especially the unnerving roar of bomber planes in the distance accentuating the horror taking place in the isolated villa. The villains in the film are even scarier than the Wicked Witch in *The Wizard of Oz*.

The ending of *Salò* actually made me misty-eyed, something that almost never happens unless it's from laughing. After all the victims and torturers are dead from rape, suicide, or murder, two Fascist guards are left to themselves. Looking somehow still innocent, but terminally bored, one asks the other to dance, and the film ends with the bewildered soldiers optimistically dancing a clumsy fox-trot. The Catholic Church ought to make Pasolini's birthday a Holy Day of Obligation.

A Cold Wind in August (1961, Alexander Singer). The very first cult film I remember, *A Cold Wind in August* may not have been a cult film anywhere else in the United States, but it played forever in Baltimore. Every time an art house would book a flop, they'd yank it and bring back *Cold Wind* in much the same way *Harold and Maude* is used today.

Since I saw the film more than twenty years ago and never again, my memory of it is quite hazy. Lola Albright (in a smashing performance) plays an over-the-hill stripper who seduces a teenage boy—a sort of poor man's Marlon Brando, played by Scott Marlowe (what a great name). Lola really gets turned on. Natch, he eventually leaves her for girls his own age and poor Lola becomes an anxiety-ridden chicken queen. It's a very method actor–type film, but what I remember most are Lola Albright's gold lamé Spring-o-later high heels, which I copied and stole for Divine to wear in many of my films.

Mademoiselle (1966, Tony Richardson). The wildest screenplay I can remember written by none other than Saint Jean Genet himself. In a remote French farming village lives

a frustrated school mistress (Jeanne Moreau) whose suppressed sexual desires explode into secret wanton acts of
violence. She delights in smashing birds' nests, poisoning the
farm animals' drinking water, drowning pigs, and setting
fire to her neighbors' houses, all in the name of sexual gratification. But the village blames the new stud in town for all
her mayhem, so Jeanne springs into action. She lures him
into a field and, in what is easily the most startling scene in
the film, seduces him by crawling on all fours like a dog and
licking his hands and boots. That accomplished, Jeanne
immediately cries rape and the villagers stone him to death.
A heroine only Jean Genet could have imagined in this midnight movie way before its time.

Lancelot du Lac (1974, Robert Bresson). Another maddening art film that really impressed me. Bresson meets the
Knights of the Round Table, sort of, since this film is told
almost entirely in close-ups or medium shots of armor, helmets, boots, horses' hooves, and very, very few human faces.
In fact, although it seems like a cast of thousands, it is actually only a handful playing many different roles. Since you
are introduced to a character from a rear view or by their
footwear, Bresson could really save money by having one
actor play twenty different parts.

If there ever was an antistar movie, this is it. Students of
film budgets ought to watch this great screen economy at
work and marvel at what the Screen Actors Guild might
think. I saw this film opening night at the Baltimore Film Festival, at which Mayor William Donald Schaefer was in attendance. I'll never forget his face at the end of the screening as
he hurriedly left the theater when asked his opinion of the
film—"Oh . . . well . . . it was okay . . . really not my kind of
picture. I liked *Patton*."

Anything by Fassbinder. Without a doubt (to me, at
least) Fassbinder was the most talented director of his day.

Anybody who idolizes Douglas Sirk is A-OK in my book. I've seen about twenty-five of his films and love all but one, *Effi Briest*.

His best are the ones he also wrote: *Katzelmacher*, with most of the early Fassbinder group sitting on a wall and bitching about foreigners; *Why Does Herr R. Run Amok?*, a film that gives new meaning to how awful everyday normal family life must be; *Beware the Holy Whore*, the thinly disguised story of the hell of making any movie that Fassbinder directs; *The Bitter Tears of Petra von Kant*, mean lesbians taunt one another while ending a neurotic affair; *Fox and His Friends*, chic homosexual falls in love with carnival worker and tries to teach him manners; and his best film of all, *In a Year of 13 Moons*, a relentlessly despairing view of the life and times of a married male who gets a sex-change operation for no other reason than because someone he admires told him, "You'd be okay if you were a broad."

Fassbinder had the reputation of being quite difficult to deal with in real life, but anyone who made as many films as his years on earth (especially if they're all good) deserves the privilege of being a true monster. If Fassbinder ever got any sleep, maybe his genius would have evaporated.

12

Why I Love Christmas

Being a traditionalist, I'm a rabid sucker for Christmas. In July I'm already worried that there are only 146 shopping days left. "What are you getting me for Christmas?" I carp to fellow bathers who haven't even decided what to do for Labor Day. As each month follows, I grow more and more obsessed. Around October I startle complete strangers by bursting into my off-key rendition of "Joy to the World." I'm always the Little Drummer Boy for Halloween, a grouchy one at that, since the inconsiderate stores haven't even put up their Christmas decorations yet. November 1st kicks off the jubilee of consumerism, and I'm so riddled with the holiday season that the mere mention of a stocking stuffer sexually arouses me.

By December I'm deep in Xmas psychosis, and only then do I allow myself the luxury of daydreaming my favorite childhood memory: dashing through the snow, laughing all the way (ha-ha-ha) to Grandma's house to find that the fully decorated tree has fallen over and pinned her underneath. My candy-colored memories have run through the projector of my mind so many times that they are almost in 3-D. That awful pause before my parents rushed to free her, my own stunned silence as I dared not ask if Granny's gifts to us had been damaged, and the wondrous, glorious sight of the now semicrooked tree, with balls broken, being begrudgingly hoisted back to its proper position of adoration. "O Christmas tree! O Christmas tree!" I started shrieking at the top of my lungs in an insane fit of childhood hyperventilation before being silenced by a glare from my parents that could have stopped a train. This tableau was never mentioned again, and my family pretended it never happened. But *I* remember— boy, do I remember!

If you don't have yourself a merry little Christmas, you might as well kill yourself. Every waking second should be spent in Christmas compulsion; career, love affairs, marriages, and all the other clutter of daily life must take a backseat to this holiday of holidays. As December 25th fast approaches, the anxiety and pressure to experience "happiness" are all part of the ritual. If you can't maintain the spirit, you're either a rotten Communist or badly in need of a psychiatrist. No wonder you don't have any friends.

Of course, You-Know-Who was supposed to have been born on Christmas, but the real Holy Trinity is God the Father, the Son, and the Holy Santa Claus. You don't see fake Josephs and Marys in department stores asking kids what they want, do you? Face it, mangers are downwardly mobile. True, swiping a sheep or a wise man for your apartment from a local church is always good for a cheap thrill and invariably gets you in the paper the next day. And Madalyn Murray O'Hair (the publicity-crazed atheist saint) always gets a rise by successfully demanding in court the removal of Nativity scenes from her state capital on Christmas Eve. But we all know who the real God is, don't we? That's right, the Supreme One, Santa Claus.

But if you think about it, Santa Claus is directly responsible for heroin addiction. Innocent children are brainwashed into believing the first big lie their parents ever tell them, and when the truth finally hits, they never believe them again. All the stern warnings on the perils of drugs carry the same credibility as flying reindeer or fat men in your chimney. But I love Santa Claus anyway: all legends have feet of clay. Besides, he's a boon to the unemployed. Where else can drunks and fat people get temporary work? And if you're a child molester—eureka! the perfect job: clutching youngsters' fannies and chuckling away, all the while knowing what *you'd* like to give them.

Of course, to many, Santa is an erotic figure, and for these lucky revelers, the Christmas season is a smorgasbord of raw sex. Some people just go for a man in a uniform. Inventive entrepreneurs should open a leather bar called the Pole where dominant wrinkle fetishists could dress like old St. Nick and passive gerontophiliacs could get on all fours and take the whip like good reindeer. Inhaling poppers and climbing down mock chimneys or opening sticks 'n' stones from the red-felt master could complete the sex-drenched atmosphere of the first S&M Xmas bar.

You could even get fancy about it. Why hasn't Bloomingdale's or Tiffany's tried a fancy Santa? Deathly pale, this never-too-thin-or-too-rich Kris Kringle, dressed in head-to-toe unstructured, oversize Armani, could pose on a throne, bored and elegant, and every so often deign to let a rich little brat sit *near* his lap before dismissing his wishes with a condescending "Oh, darling, you don't *really* want that, do you?"

Santa has always been the ultimate movie star. Forget *White Christmas*, *It's a Wonderful Life*, and all the other hackneyed trash. Go for the classics: *Silent Night, Bloody Night, Black Christmas*, or the best seasonal film of all time, *Christmas Evil* ("He'll sleigh you"). This true cinematic masterpiece only played theatrically for a few seconds but it's now available on videocassette and no holiday family get-together is complete without it. It's about a man completely consumed by Christmas. His neurosis first rears its ugly head as he applies shaving cream to his face, looks in the mirror, hallucinates a white beard, and begins to imagine that he *is* Santa Claus. He gets a job in a toy factory, starts snooping and spying on the neighborhood children, and then rushes home to feverishly make notes in his big red book: "Jimmy was a good boy today," or "Peggy was a bad little girl." He starts cross-dressing as Claus and lurks around people's roofs ready to take the plunge. Finally, he actually gets stuck in a nearby chimney and awakens the family in his struggle. Mom and Dad go insane when they find a fat lunatic in their fireplace, but the kids are wild with glee. Santa has no choice but to kill these Scroogelike parents with the razor-sharp star decorating the top of their tree. As he flees a neighborhood lynch mob, the children come to his rescue and defy their distraught parents by forming a human ring of protection around him. Finally, pushed to the limits of Clausmania, he leaps into his van/sleigh and it takes off flying over the moon as he psy-chotically and happily shrieks, "On Dancer! On Prancer! On Donner and Vixen!" I wish I had kids. I'd make them watch it every year and if they didn't like it they'd be punished.

Pre-holiday activities are the foreplay of Christmas. Nat-urally, Christmas cards are your first duty, and you *must* send one (with a personal, handwritten message) to every single person you ever met, no matter how briefly. If this common courtesy is not reciprocated, never speak to the person again. Keep computerized records of violators and hold the grudge forever; don't even attend their funeral.

Of course, you must *make* your own cards by hand. "I don't have time," you may whine, but since the whole purpose of life is Christmas, you'd better *make* time, buster. We Christ-mas zealots are rather demanding when it comes to the basic requirements of holiday behavior. "But I can't think of any-thing . . ." is usually the next excuse, but cut those people off in mid-sentence. It's easy to be creative at Christmastime. One year I had a real cute idea that was easy to design. I bought a cheap generic card of Joseph and Mary holding the Baby Jesus and superimposed Charles Manson's face in place of the homeless infant's. Inside I kept the message "He is born." Everybody told me they loved it and some even said they saved it. (For the record, I'm against donating your cards to nursing homes after Christmas. One would think that after all these years on earth, senior citizens would have had a chance to make a friend or two on their own. Don't do it!) This season, I'm dying to produce my dream card that I've wanted for years. I'll be sitting in a Norman Rockwell–style Christmas scene, dressed in robe and slippers, opening my gifts moments before I notice a freak fire that has begun in the tissue paper and is licking and spreading to the tree.

Go deeply in debt over Christmas shopping. Always spend in exact correlation to how much you like the recipient. Aunt Mary I love about $6.50 worth; Uncle Jim—well, at least he got his teeth fixed—$8. If your Christmas comes and goes without declaring bankruptcy, I feel sorry for you—you are a person with not enough love inside.

You can never buy too many presents. If you said "Excuse me" to me on a transit bus, you're on *my* list. I wrap gifts for nonexistent people in case somebody I barely know hands me a present and I'm unprepared to return this gesture. Even though I'm the type who infuriates others by saying, "Oh, I finished my shopping months ago," as they frantically try to make last-minute decisions, I like to go into the stores at the height of Christmasmania. Everyone is in a horrid mood, and you can see the overburdened, underpaid temporary help having nervous breakdowns. I always write down their badge numbers and report them for being grumpy.

If you're a criminal, Christmas is an extra-special time for you and your family. Shoplifting is easier and cars in parking lots are loaded with presents for your children. Since every-one steals the checks you must leave for the mailman and garbagemen, I like to leave little novelty items, like letter bombs. Luckily, I live in a bad neighborhood, so I don't have to worry; the muggers live in my building and go to the rich neighborhoods to rob. If you're quick, you can even steal the muggers' loot as they unload the car. Every child in my district seems to get rollerskates for Christmas, and it's music to my ears to hear the sudden roar of an approaching gang on skates, tossing back and forth like a hot potato a purse they've just snatched.

"Santa Claus Is a Black Man" is my favorite Christmas carol, but I also like *The Chipmunks' Christmas Album*, the Barking Dogs' "Jingle Bells," and "Frosty the Snowman" by the Ronettes. If you're so filled with holiday cheer you can't stand it, try calling your friends and going caroling yourself. Especially if you're old, a drug addict, an alcoholic, or obviously homosexual and have a lot of effeminate friends. Go in packs. If you are black, go to a prissy white neighborhood. Ring doorbells, and when the Father Knows Best–type family answers, start screeching hostilely your favorite carol. Watch their faces. There's nothing they can do. It's not illegal. Maybe they'll give you a present.

Always be prepared if someone asks you what you want for Christmas. Give brand names, the store that sells the merchandise, and, if possible, exact model numbers so they can't go wrong. Be the type who's impossible to buy for so that they have to get what you want. Here was my 1985 list and I had checked it twice: the long-out-of-print paperback *The Indiana Torture Slaying*, the one-sheet for the film *I Hate Your Guts*, and a subscription to *Corrections Today*, the trade paper for prison wardens. If you owe someone money, now is the time to pay him back, mentioning at the same time a perfect gift suggestion. If you expect to be receiving a Christmas stocking as a forerunner to a present, tell the giver right off the bat that you don't go for razor blades, deodorants, or any of the other common little sundries but anticipate stocking stuffers that are original, esoteric, and perfectly suited to you and you alone.

It helps to be a collector, so the precedent is set on what to expect as a gift. For years friends have treated me to the toy annually selected by the Consumer Affairs Committee of Americans for Democratic Action as the "worst toy" to give you child at Christmastime. "Gobbles, the Garbage-Eating Goat" started my collection. "That crazy eating goat," reads the delightful package, and in small print, "Contains: One realistic goat with head that goes up and down. Comes complete with seven pieces of pretend garbage." This Kenner Discovery Time toy's instructions are priceless. "Gobbles loves to eat garbage when he's hungry, and he's ALWAYS hungry. (1) Hold Gobbles' mouth open by the beard. Stuff a piece of pretend garbage straight into his mouth and (2) pump the tail until the garbage disappears." It ends with an ominous warning, "Feed Gobbles *only* the garbage that comes with the toy," and in even smaller print, "If you need additional garbage, we will, as a service, send it to you direct. For 14 pieces of garbage send $1 (check or money order; sorry, no C.O.D.) to . . ." I can't tell you the hours of fun I've had with Gobbles. Sometimes when I'm very bored, Gobbles and I get naked and play-play.

Over the years my collection has grown. There's "My Puppy Puddles" ("You can make him drink water, wet in his tray, and kiss you"). "Baby Cry and Dry," about whom the watchdog group warned: "Take her out of the box and she smells, the odor won't go away," and "Baby Cry for You" ("The tears don't just drop out, they whoosh out in a three-foot stream"). Of course, I still covet the winner of the first annual prize (before my collection began)—a guillotine for dolls. "Take that, Barbie." "Off with your head, Betsy Wetsy!"

No matter what you think of your presents, each must be

answered with an immediate thank-you note. Thinking of what to write can be tricky, especially for distant relatives who send you a card with two crisp $1 bills inside. Be honest in your reply—"Dear Uncle Walt. Thank you for the $2. I bought a pack of Kools and then put the change in an especially disgusting peep show. It was fun!" or "Dear Aunt Lulu, I was thrilled to receive your kind gift of $5. I immediately bought some PCP with it. Unfortunately, I had a bad reaction, stabbed my sister, set the house on fire, and got taken to the hospital for the criminally insane. Maybe you could come visit me? Love, Your Nephew."

I always have an "office party" every year and invite my old friends, business associates, and any snappy criminals who have been recently paroled. I reinforce all my chairs, since for some reason many of my guests are very fat, and after a few splintered antiques, I've learned my lesson. I used to throw the party on Christmas Eve, but so many guests complained of hideous hangovers I had to move up the date. No more moaning and dry heaving under their parents' tree the next day as their brothers and sisters give them dirty looks for prematurely ejaculating the Christmas spirit.

I usually invite about a hundred people and the guests know I expect each to get everyone else a present. Ten thousand gifts! When they're ripped open at midnight, you can see Christmas dementia at its height. One thing that pushes me off the deep end is party crashers. I've solved the problem by hiring a doorman who pistol-whips anyone without an invitation, but in the old days, crashers actually got inside. How rude! At Christmas, of all times, when visions of sugarplums are dancing orgiastically through my head. One even brought her mother—how touching. "GET OUT!" I snarled after snatching out of her hand the bottle of liquor that she falsely assumed would gain her (*and* her goddamn mother) entry.

I always show a film in one room: *Wedding Trough* (about

a man who falls in love with a pig and then eats it), or *Kitten with a Whip* (Ann-Margret and John Forsythe), or *What Sex Am I?* (a clinical documentary about a sex-change operation). When it's finally time for the guests to leave, I blatantly get in bed and go to sleep; they know they better get home, Santa is on his way.

Christmas Day is like an orgasm that never stops. Happiness and good cheer should be throbbing in your veins. Swilling eggnog, scarfing turkey, and wildly ripping open presents with your family, one must pause to savor the feeling of inner peace. Once it's over, you can fall apart.

Now is the time for suicide if you are so inclined. All sorts of neuroses are permitted. Depression and feelings that it somehow wasn't good enough should be expected. There's nothing to do! Go to a bad movie? You can't leave the house between now and January 1 because it's unsafe; the national highways are filled with drunks unwinding and frantically trying to get away from their families. Returning gifts is not only rude but psychologically dangerous—if you're not careful you might glimpse the scum of the earth, cheap bastards who shop at after-Christmas sales to save a few bucks. What can you look forward to? January 1, the Feast of the Circumcision, perhaps the most unappetizing High Holiday in the Catholic Church? Cleaning up that dirty, dead, expensive Christmas tree that is now an instant out-of-season fire hazard? There is only one escape from post-Christmas depression—the thought that in four short weeks it's time to start all over again. What're ya gonna get me?

13

How *Not* to Make a Movie

I've always wanted to sell out. The problem is nobody wanted to buy me. Ever since I was a toddler I longed to be a film director (or a mad bomber), so I was lucky not to waste time floundering around in youth looking for a vocation. If you're cursed with the movie bug, you're forced to decide early if you want to remain independent or go Hollywood. There are no rules on either path. It's a real-life version of that kids' board game Chutes and Ladders. Just when you think you have it all figured out, along comes some industry hotshot or eccentric entrepreneur to scramble your plans in a minute. "Make it more commercial," the studio bigwigs scream, but the independent producers growl back, "being original is what really counts." Maybe the solution a distributor friend suggested is the answer: Take the budget of the film you want to make, divide it by the estimated number of people who would pay to see it, add one million, and charge accordingly. Bresson's *L'Argent*, admission $62.75; *Rocky XX*, 42¢. Then everyone would make money and be happy. Isn't that what being commercial is all about?

It used to be the way to start out was to make a low-budget exploitation film. Look at Coppola (*Dementia 13*) or Scorsese (*Boxcar Bertha*). But now it's not so simple. Hollywood has co-opted the slash-and-trash formula, and these days even garbage needs a big budget. It's not nearly as much fun. A $10-million version of *The Corpse Grinders* just wouldn't have the charm of the original. Another problem is that there are few taboos left; once you have freedom there's no way to attack. Splatter is already old hat. It's impossible to imagine more gore than the Hollywood remake of *The Thing*, but once you've seen it, so what? A glimpse of pubic hair in the old days would guarantee lines around the block, but a spread-eagle Linda Evans in the near future is not impossible to imagine. You can always think of ways to offend (AIDS, sickle-cell anemia, and rape jokes) but this would hardly be daring, only stupid. Maybe the Golden Age of Trash is coming to an end.

The true exploitation films of the eighties are TV-issue movies. It must really be hard to be a teenager these days; as soon as you think of a problem to get on your parents' nerves, the networks produce "entertainment" explaining that you're really OK. We've had it all: homosexuality, mercy killing, wife beating, matri- and patricide, even child abuse was trendy for a while. As much as I try to understand all deviant behavior, this last one always mystifies me. Since everybody knows that the whole reason to have sex is because cigarettes taste better afterward, don't these molesters feel foolish being there naked as a six-year-old hacks away on his first Lucky Strike?

Farrah Fawcett, of course, has made a career out of being abused. Ever notice how she was slammed by the critics until the actors started doing it themselves? First she was raped off Broadway, then beaten on network television. Isn't the ultimate Farrah role that of Kitty Genovese, the unfortunate woman who was stabbed to death in New York and became famous because none of her neighbors helped her or called the police?

How about a socially redeeming TV movie concerning a happy, healthy homosexual living in the West Village surrounded by well-adjusted friends and emotionally supported by liberal parents who suddenly finds himself attracted to women. "Help me," he begs horrified heterophobics. "Take it easy. We know a great psychiatrist who specializes in these problems," his concerned parents plead. "It's only a phase." Or Wayne Newton as a lesbian male impersonator who's had so many sex changes back and forth that he/she starts a fashion trend with the layered look in sexual parts.

The newest and most maligned of genres, the "Teenage Coming of Age" picture, was bankable for a while. It's fashionable to hate these films, but a few of them I've liked, especially *Heaven Help Us*. I loved *The Breakfast Club* for all the wrong reasons, and wished it had been like an old Warhol film with an eight-hour running time so the audience would feel as if they too were trapped in detention hall along with the characters. Hollywood kept cranking out these films but they made a mistake in not underestimating the intelligence of the American public enough. Forget high school; grade school should have been next. A rip-off of *The Breakfast Club* that took place in nursery school would have been even better. Spoiled brats whining over lost fingerpaints, tricycle flats, and losing at Pin-the-Tail-on-the-Donkey would have sent the grosses through the roof.

Maybe "instant movies" are the answer. I like to think I made the first of the teen-suicide movies when I tested a camera and shot *The Diane Linkletter Story* as an improvisational joke, the same day I read about the tragedy in the paper. Rene Cardona, Jr. and Sr. (father and son team), the top directors in this field, made *Survive*, a cheapie version of the Andes-airplane-crash-survivor-cannibalism case before Hollywood had a chance to shoot the same story (the bestseller *Alive*) they had just shelled out big bucks for. They also made *Guyana, Cult of the Damned*, and had the nerve to announce plans to produce *Kill the Shah*, *Boat People*, and *Hostages* (who were then still detained by the Ayatollah). The perfect exercise for film school would be to read the morning paper and complete a film on the most sensational story before the evening edition hit the streets. Imagine the surprise of passersby on their way home from work seeing a film playing in their neighborhood on a subject that only entered their consciousness that very morning.

You'd think sequels would be safe but they're not. My favorites are the last ones in the series just before it dies out: *Airport '79—The Concorde* with Charo's immortal line—"You mis-conscrew me"; *The Final Conflict,* the most ludicrous of the *Omen*s; and *Emmanuelle IV* in 3-D, where she goes to a sex clinic and is mistakenly turned back into a virgin. All of these are art in reverse. I look forward to the last of the *Friday the 13th*s when Jason goes to Hollywood and hacks up fifteen— that's right, fifteen—of your favorite old Hollywood stars in cameo victim roles. Yvonne De Carlo with a knife, Rudy Vallee with an ice pick, maybe even Esther Williams with a chain saw.

But when I tried to make the sequel to *Pink Flamingos* nobody would give me the money. "Can you give us something we can *admit* we like?" said one studio executive who claimed to have laughed "out loud" while reading the script. "Columbia Pictures," he explained, "couldn't exactly have a board meeting and announce their new product by showing stockholders giant photos of Divine." "Why not?" I demanded. "If you took the ratio between cost and gross of the first *Pink Flamingos* and applied it to a Hollywood budget, you'd have a blockbuster." "Well, you can't have shit in a Hollywood film," he countered, perplexed that he had to spell it out. You could have fooled me, I thought as I bit my tongue and instead blurted, "A sequel to *Pink Flamingos* without a turd is like *Jaws* without a shark. Audiences wouldn't stand for it!" No such logic helped. *Pink Flamingos Meets Emmanuelle in Bangkok Beneath the Valley of the Ultra-Vixens, Next-to-Last Chapter in 3-D, Part 6* will have to remain unfilmed, festering in my vision until maybe one day I turn it into a novel. Product shortage is what I'm all about.

Being "controversial" is a big help if you're independent. When Media Home Entertainment was scheduled to release four of my films on videocassette, they had the package designed, a great ad campaign ready ("Let's get trash back into the homes where it belongs"), and I was all set to go on a promotional tour. When the company's salesmen and jobbers in the Midwest saw the product they reportedly flipped out and refused to sell them. Mutiny. I was crushed. But because they had already sent out the press releases announcing the cassettes, the video reviewers had a better story than if the videos had been released without a hitch. So another company, Continental Video, offered more money than we had with the first deal. Now if this had been Hollywood, the tapes would never have been released, you would be as good as dead for tarnishing the company image, and probably wouldn't even be invited to the D-list screening of *Bolero*.

It's safe and even advisable to imitate past Hollywood hits when you're trying to get studio backing, but never try and copy an independent if you're going that route. A rip-off of *The Gods Must Be Crazy* or *Stranger Than Paradise* will get you nowhere, but the marketplace may be able to support five or six imitation *Star Wars*. "You're in the ultimate *Catch-22* position," one friendly studio executive told me off the record. "We all know your work and would gladly pay to go to your premieres; your name gets you in the door, but it also keeps you out for the very reason of your success." There are a million "vice presidents" in Hollywood and their jobs are safe as long as they say "no"; it's a tentative "yes" that sets in panic.

"Pitching" is a necessary skill if you ever want to make a

film. Why this isn't a credited course in film schools is beyond me. Independently, it consists of bothering any family relative with money and going to parties to meet rich people. In the past, I've felt like an encyclopedia salesman; I even acted out the entire movie, playing every part for a potential backer. Usually it takes months of "meetings," even years, before they'll decide to give you the money. In Hollywood it's much better. You go in, have about fifteen minutes to pitch, and they let you know in a few days. If you get the first of many green lights, they give you a lot of money to go home and "develop" the project. You both know that the chances of it ending up on screen are slim and, if it does, it will have only the slightest resemblance to your original idea.

My first "pitching experience" in Hollywood came when I tried to get the job of director for *A Confederacy of Dunces*, a book I loved and the only project I'd ever been interested in that I didn't write. The meeting seemed to go OK; the producer listened politely to my ideas, but I never heard from him again. He never even gave me the official "no." It wasn't until about a year later that I figured out why. I had left this executive a copy of my book which included a photo of myself and a mass murderer I had befriended in my never-ending interest in prison rehabilitation. Unfortunately, he had killed one of this producer's best friends. I felt really awful. And, natch, I didn't get the job. It might have been the single most disastrous "meeting" to ever take place in Hollywood, but then I guess that all directors have their stories.

On another "pitching" trip, I had appointments with several of the studios. Since one of my projects was about the day fat people take over the world, I prayed I didn't walk into an office and see an overweight producer. It would be really embarrassing to say, "Nice to meet you. I've got this great comedy about fat people," as he or she eyed me maliciously over a big bowl of mashed potatoes. I soon ditched this project when another producer told me she could hardly push it with her boss, who was a California health nut, eternally tanned and a fat bigot.

In another studio I tried an alternate idea I had (the one I'm working on now) and it seemed to work. Hollywood actually liked my idea. "Get out quickly," agents advise at the first sign of approval, "before you say something to make them change their minds." The studio bigwigs asked to screen *Polyester*, the last film I had made. Since it received mainstream positive reviews, made money, and looked pretty good considering the tiny (by Hollywood standards) budget, I figured it would be the perfect résumé. But it turned out to be every independent filmmaker's nightmare. The executive kept looking at his watch, griped, "You think *this* is funny?" and left after fifteen minutes. Needless to say, they "passed" on the project. I love these Hollywood terms. If a film opens "softly" it means it was a big bomb. "Passed" is a polite way of saying, "Think of the letter *M*; think of the next two letters in the alphabet and apply them. *NO!* Get out!"

"Pitching" never really ends no matter how big you are. Once in Baltimore I attended a financial get-together for local fat cats to raise money for a film called *Wilderness*. The budget was $20 million. It starred Richard Dreyfuss and was to be directed by John Frankenheimer (*Seven Days in May, The Manchurian Candidate, Birdman of Alcatraz*). There he was, doing the same thing I had been doing for years—hustling money. God, it never ends! The only difference was that he had part of the pitch on video, much fancier financial prospectives, and the potential backers got a gourmet meal. I usually just offered them a cigarette.

"Casting" is very important in getting a film financed since even one "name" is enough to guarantee a nontheatrical sale to Uganda or some such important international ancillary market. Try hiring brothers and sisters of famous stars (Joey

Travolta, Kevin Dillon) and hope that nobody in Tunisia knows the difference. Independently, cast and crew will sometimes work for a small salary if you give them "points" in the film's profits. I never understood why you couldn't be fair and reverse this custom and ask for the salaries *back* if the project *loses* money.

The ultimate star of a non-Hollywood movie would be Liberace, the personification of everything I believe in pushed to the *nth* degree. He'd be perfect for a horror film. There was even a rumor in the gossip columns (hotly denied) that he was signed to play the lead in the sequel to *The Texas Chain Saw Massacre*. He'd be absolutely perfect. I met him and he's really scary. Your first reaction when you stick out your hand to shake is to involuntarily scream when you see him up close. His facial skin is pulled so tight that he can't *not* smile. He's *Mr. Sardonicus* for real. Picture him chasing Drew Barrymore across a swamp with a buzzing chain saw and you can envision a megahit of staggering proportions.

In Hollywood, the real stars are all in animation. Alvin and the Chipmunks don't throw star fits, don't demand custom-designed Winnebagos, and are a breeze at costume fittings. Cruella DeVille, Gorgo, Rainbow Brite, Gus-Gus, Uncle Scrooge, and the Care Bears all are superstars and they don't have drug problems, marital difficulties, or paternity suits to blacken their images. They don't age, balk at promoting, or sass highly paid directors. Plus, you can market them to death and they never feel exploited. I'd like to do a big-budget snuff film starring every last one of them.

Naturally, I have hundreds of fantasy projects that I don't even bother pitching because I know they'll never get made. *Divine Meets Francis the Talking Mule*, a bestiality love story for mature children where Francis turns queer and helps Divine pick out her evening gowns. Or a remake of *Persona* starring Liv Ullmann and Benji, "together at last on the screen." Or a documentary where Manson and all of his one-time Family are reunited for one afternoon in a tacky L.A. banquet hall. Some are now Jesus freaks, some rehabilitated, while others are still loyal to the cause. Imagine the drama, the tension, and with the title of *The Big Kill*, it would be commercial as well. If this isn't "high concept," what is?

Film students waste too much time studying "masterpieces." *Hit and Run Filmmaking, Avoiding the Unions*, or *To Hell with Completion Bonds* would be a much more practical syllabus. Professors should concentrate on explaining how to set up a limited partnership with ten cocaine-addicted dentists, or faking talent insurance forms with doctors when your leading lady weighs over five hundred pounds or is addicted to morning glory seeds. "Air" should be a textbook, since this term is widely accepted by the industry to describe the unchangeable, rip-off factor in this cash business. Do film students know that you can hire a "checker" to go around to the theaters, pay admission, and hand count the customers to see if the official box-office report reflects the truth? Do they also know that some theaters figure out who the "checkers" are and pay them more to lie? Do buffs who profess to love the cinema more than life check their torn ticket stubs to see if the serial number matches the original? Otherwise theater employees are ripping off their favorite directors by reselling the tickets and pocketing the price. Do graduate students in high-powered film schools know that trendy nightclubs will pay the entire cost of a fancy party for your premiere so they get their club in the papers the next day? Is any real *practical* advice taught today? Repeated screenings of *Rashomon* won't help your career. Screen a film that played everywhere in the world, had a profitable video release, and made money. Analyze what progressed from the moment of conception to the actual distribution of profits. Pick a real film. A practical one. How about *C.H.U.D.*? It's pretty good. The mysterious title stands for *Cannibalistic Humanoid Underground Dwellers* or, in plain English, monsters who live in the sewers of New York. Besides being the perfect film for study, it can drive home the message that these "CHUDs" ain't nothing compared to some of the people you'll have to meet in the movie business.

"But how can I actually get Hollywood to finance me?" film students always wonder. I think I have the answer. Follow this scenario and I guarantee that you will end up in Beverly Hills with your name impressively listed in the Directors Guild of America. If you want to go the studio route, firstly, write the executive of your choice and confide that you are one of his children's PCP dealers, feel guilty, and would like to discuss it with him. Once you have the appointment, dress the part. You're a film director, aren't you? Wear a beret, a monocle firmly implanted, use an extra long cigarette holder, and carry a loud-hailer. A riding crop in the other hand, if you want to be really daring. When the secretary shows you in, yell "Action," and every time the bigwig makes a point you can use to your advantage, bellow, "Cut! Print!" For some unfathomable reason, the axiom "It's easier to get $5 million than $500,000" seems to be true, so ask for $40 million right off the bat. Explain that naturally you have an army of lackeys that travel with you and they are used to the high life. Talk his language; he'll understand. Pitching your story, always compare it to a recent hit, since the studios never seem to remember that the biggest moneymakers were highly original in the first place. If your project is about teenagers who are prematurely aged to senility by a certain sex act and then take out their revenge by killing newborn infants, describe it as a horror film combining the best of *Cocoon* and *Back to the Future*. Once you get the development deal, complete the draft you want and then write four inferior versions and turn in the worst first. Since no matter how great your script is, they always make you do rewrites. You can save yourself some time and headaches by letting them think your script improved because of their input.

Select a crew that is either ex-cons or very sexy, preferably both. Prisoners are good for beating up union representatives snooping around the set, and if he or she is cute, you can talk them into posing for nude shots at lunch to sell to the skin magazines. Give the crew speed so they're not just loafing about. Yelling, "Dollar! Dollar! Dollar!" as the seconds tick by is a good way to remind people that filmmaking is hardly a lark. Kidnapping a major star and forcing him to do your film is a surefire way to generate excitement about your project. You won't even have to hire a unit publicist. Threatening to cut off your leading lady's ear and mail it to *Daily Variety* unless she does the fiftieth take is an effective form of actor-modification. Have some hack on the set writing up *The Making of* —— to ensure a quickie paperback sale. Make the unknown supporting actors break into film labs and steal raw stock. "You want to be a movie star, don't you? Well, let's just see how badly" is motivation enough for any aspiring thespian.

Shoot only one version of your film. Destroy any excess footage immediately, never cover yourself or some producer will barge into the editing room and suggest, "How about trying it this way?" Not having the footage is an excellent way to protect yourself if you don't have "final cut" in your contract.

Once the film is completed, four-wall theaters for your sneak previews and make *sure* you get audience reaction. Plant shills in the theater to stage fake heart attacks if it's a horror film, or hire community Casanovas to rush forward and hump the screen if it's supposed to be sexy. Better yet, bribe a nursing-home attendant to bring a terminally ill patient to your screening so he actually dies in the theater. Word of mouth will be great. Like all distributors, wildly exaggerate your initial grosses and then sell the film outright to a studio for a huge profit plus points. When the film finally has its official world premiere, get busted for all your cinematic crimes and plead "temporary insanity to celluloid." If possible, have your trial in Los Angeles, where the coverage will be peak, and pad the jury with industry types. You'll get off and Hollywood will finally respect you. The offers will come faster than a tidal wave and you'll be rolling in dough. Can an Oscar be far behind?

14

Hail Mary

With the Pope as your press agent, you are bound to stir up a little interest. But ticket buyers expecting sacrilegious outrage may be a bit disappointed with the much maligned Jean-Luc Godard film *Hail Mary*. From all the hoopla, I was half expecting a topless Mary on a donkey, writhing her way to Bethlehem, giving rosary jobs to every Tom, Dick, and Harry along the way. If all the fanatical Catholics who are going so berserk over *Hail Mary* (and giving it millions of dollars' worth of free publicity) would bother seeing the film, I doubt they'd still be awake at the closing credits. After all, it *is* Godard. A friend in California still refuses to ever attend a movie with me after I dragged him to a triple feature of Godard films more than ten years ago. We all know Godard can be difficult, obscure, even pretentious. Yes, *Hail Mary* is all three. But it is also hysterically funny. It's my favorite foreign film since *The Moon in the Gutter* (the *Beyond the Valley of the Dolls* of "art" pictures). Go see it with someone you've sinned with. Buy them an indulgence instead of flowers.

Anybody who has seen Godard's last few films (*Every Man for Himself, Passion, First Name—Carmen, Detective*) knows he is a great wit, screwball, and eccentric revolutionary all rolled into one. He gives genius a good name. But who would have ever thought he was holy to boot? Well, good Lord, this film is causing the biggest stink since Cardinal Francis "Kitty"

Spellman branded *Baby Doll* a one-way ticket to hell in the fifties. Haven't censors figured out by now that the best way to stop a film is to never mention it? Did the hundred or more priests and nuns who showed up to demonstrate at the Rome premiere of *Hail Mary* think they would actually *hurt* the film's grosses? When the manager of the theater was actually beaten the next day, did they feel responsible? When Pope John Paul II rose to the bait and denounced the film and led a special prayer ceremony "to repair the outrage inflicted on the Holy Virgin," did he not realize he was guaranteeing Godard an audience for this film much larger than for his past efforts? When Triumph Films (a division of Columbia Pictures, which is owned by Coca-Cola) got cold feet and dumped their planned American release of *Hail Mary*, were they really worried ticket buyers would switch to Pepsi? ("They should drink Coca-Cola anyway," Godard politely quipped at the packed press conference following the press screening at the New York Film Festival.) And did Cardinal John O'Connor of New York and the army of holy-water-throwing demonstrators not realize they were a press agent's dream who turned an obscure French film into an "event"?

Is *Hail Mary* really blasphemous? Can it top the amazing climax of Buñuel's much-acclaimed *Viridiana*, where an orgy of filthy beggars riot through a house, listen to Handel's *Messiah*, and are "photographed" by an old woman obscenely lifting her skirts, as they gather around a table drunkenly and freeze into the infamous parody of da Vinci's *Last Supper?* Or Jerzy Kawalerowicz's *Mother Joan of the Angels*, which tells the tale of a priest sent to exorcise the demons out of a possessed convent who is instead drawn to the earthy charm of Mother Joan, decides to take on her sins, and murders two innocent people for the "love" of his nun? Even the 1951 Supreme Court was caught up in the act of determining what is sacrilegious and decided *The Miracle* was entitled to constitutional protection. The story of a young peasant girl seduced by a vagrant she imagines is Saint Joseph may have raised the hackles of the clergy at the time, but the scene where the villagers taunt the "saint" and crown her with a wash-basin halo is now one for the history books. Some even objected to Saint Pier Paolo ("I am a Catholic. I am a Communist. I am a homosexual") Pasolini's *The Gospel According to St. Matthew* because it portrayed Mary as "ordinary" or "cold." Like taste, blasphemy is in the eye of the beholder. Wouldn't Richard Gere as *King David* or Mary Tyler Moore as a nun in the Elvis vehicle *Change of Habit* be considered blasphemous in some communities? The bottom line: Would Flannery O'Connor have liked *Hail Mary?* I wish this one sane Catholic, whose writings on dogma made sense, were still around to explain it all to me.

Godard's "Mary" works in her father's gas station and is something of a basketball buff. Joseph is a cab driver. Before you can say, "The Lord is with thee," the Archangel Gabriel arrives to watch over Joseph (in yet another obsessively beautiful shot of an airplane that seems to be a signature of Godard's later films). Gabriel is accompanied by a weird little girl who is his secretary and looks like the spooky child in Fassbinder's *Chinese Roulette.* Together they do all sorts of surreal things, such as tying Gabriel's shoe, each with a hand on one lace. Mary, a normal girl if there ever was one, feels pregnant, imagines the upcoming event, and, since she has had no career plans in this direction, is naturally ambivalent in her feelings. Joseph has never slept with Mary, so he is skeptical when Gabriel tells him she is with child and doesn't believe Mary's pleas of "I sleep with no one." "By God, it's incredible," Joseph says with a straight face. "You must be sleeping around guys with big cocks." Mary goes to the

gynecologist, asks, "Do souls have bodies?" and he confirms
her worst fears. "Tell Joseph," Mary begs.

Mary starts going a little crazy with holiness. She dreams
fragments of prayers and thrashes around in the bathtub
trying to rid herself of impure desire. At least she doesn't have
morning sickness. Joseph is also having a rough time. Mary
berates him for being stupid (he reads to his dog and has never
heard of Shakespeare), and Gabriel and his assistant hassle
him for being a jerk and not knowing how to dress properly.
Worse yet, Mary spurns all his sexual advances. "Why does
my body repel you?" Joseph gripes before losing his temper
and smacking her around. To shut him up, she finally lets him
feel her leg only briefly, and I guess theologians will have to
debate if this was Mary's first venial sin. "Can I see you
naked only once?" Joseph pleads. "I'll only look." Mary can't
sleep. After all, she didn't *ask* to be the Virgin Mother. "Why
me?" you keep expecting her to scream. Finally, Mary relents
and allows Joseph to watch her undress, but no "Roman
hands" for this girl. Joseph: "I love you" (reaching for her
naked body). Mary: "No!" Suddenly, Gabriel appears out of
nowhere and wrestles Joseph away from temptation, shouting,
"It's the law!" All intercut with beautiful cloud shots, the
sun, the moon, trains zooming by, accented by an experimental sound track like no other—insects screaming, intense
wind; better than Dolby. Eventually, Joseph is allowed to put
his head on Mary's swollen stomach and he becomes resigned
to his role: "I never touch you. I'll stay."

Mary begins intoning all sorts of lunatic inner monologues—"The Father and Mother must fuck over my body
and Lucifer will die," "God is a vampire," and other such nonsense that pushes pretension one step beyond to hilarity and,
finally, to a certain insane fluency. She keeps attending those
damn basketball games, no matter how pregnant, and, since

I have no clue as to the symbolism of those scenes, I instead meditated on the news account I read recently where a nine-month pregnant woman was busted mistakenly in a sporting goods store for shoplifting a basketball under her dress.

We never actually see the birth, but we hear a baby crying over confusing shots of planes flying, snow, and, most per-plexingly, a snowplow. Cut to a bloody cow. We see Mary's concerned father ask the new mother, "Will He call Joseph dad?" "That's life," quips Mary with her usual lack of humor. And then we *finally* see a donkey. A great donkey! Framed with reverence, the best single shot in the movie. I almost expected him to whisper in Chill Wills' voice, "Hail, Mary," but it definitely is *not* that kind of picture.

When we finally see the Kid, I was disappointed His head didn't spin around. Damien He ain't. As He grows older He does things like putting His whole head up Mary's dress. "He's too old to see you naked," Joseph warns. Crotch level, the Child asks, "What's that?" and, I swear to God, Mary answers, "Hedgery," which must be in the same family as "bush." I'm surprised she doesn't send Him to school at Summerhill. "He who is your Father may forget you, but I'll be around," Joseph lectures. When the Savior runs away, saying "I must tend to my Father's work," Joseph asks, "When will He be back?" Mary answers, in what must be the most hilarious line in the movie, "Easter."

The finale is priceless. Mary is getting into her car in a parking lot and Gabriel, whom she doesn't know, is waiting. "Madam?" he keeps repeating, but Mary's thoughts are else-where. Finally, noticing him, she absentmindedly replies, "Yes?" and he responds reverently, "Hail, Mary." I thought I would levitate out of my seat. It's the very best scene where the title is actually uttered in dialogue. Even better than Taylor and Burton saying, "*Boom!*" for no apparent reason, or

Debbie Reynolds' cinematic question of the century, "Well, *What's the Matter with Helen?*"

Mary finally lights a cigarette (far less blasphemous than Jane Fonda chain-smoking unconvincingly in *Agnes of God*), puts on lipstick, and, as we hear an angelic chorus, says, "I am of the Virgin." The camera goes in for a close-up of Mary's lips, resulting in an unintentional parody of the credits and print campaign for *The Rocky Horror Picture Show*. The End. Proceed directly to hell.

If this film sounds scandalous, believe me, it's not. Although the cinematography is incredible, the acting first-rate, and the script guaranteed to bring a smile to anyone with a sense of humor who was raised a Catholic, it is also very confusing—hardly a crossover art film to be dubbed for the suburbs. As in most Godard films, half the time I had no idea what was going on, something I wish I could say about many Hollywood films. But the general public is not going to buy it. It's the *Snuff* of art films; take the money and run before word gets out to other sensationmongers that, like *I Am Curious (Yellow)*, you have to sit through a lot in order to see what all the fuss is about.

The film *is* reverent in its own ironic way. (Some members of the Catholic press have come out and praised the film, and it supposedly won the International Catholic Cinema Office Award at the Berlin Film Festival.) *Hail Mary* actually made me, an ex-Catholic, think fondly of religion for the first time in decades. Who knows what effect *Hail Mary* will have on my own spirituality? Of all people, I never thought *Godard* might tempt me back to the Church. Now, at least, I have a new respect for the outrageousness and originality of the concept of the Immaculate Conception. Maybe I won't be as angry as I used to be when I hear childhood Catholic trauma stories, such as the one a friend named Mary (her real name) told me recently: All through the year in grade school the nuns showed the class a mysterious hole in the wall at the end of the hall. One by one, each girl was taken to peer in but forbidden to reveal what they saw. When Mary's time finally came, she apprehensively approached, stuck her head through, and saw herself reflected in a mirror across from her, framed in a nun's habit. She finally got to see herself as a nun. Did the good sister accompanying her whisper in her ear, "Hail, Mary"? I wonder.

Is supposed sacrilege the only taboo left? Now that sex and violence have been co-opted by Hollywood, is this the only way to get a rise out of the audience looking for a new kind of exploitation picture? Will there be "spin-off" sacrilegious movies? Will Russ Meyer do *The Mary Magdalene Story*? Will Paul Schrader have to deal with the heirs of *Judas*? Can I do the American remake of *Hail Mary*? Divine would be great in the role, and if any old-fashioned gay gentlemen in the audience cried out, "Oh, Mary!" it could start a whole new trend in modern-day prayers. Oh, Mary. Hail, Mary.

15

Celebrity Burnout

I'm sick of celebrities. You know who I mean. I can't even bear to say their names out loud. Read my lips: the one who shaved her armpits and got married under a helicopter attack. Or the one who appeared nude in *Playgirl* magazine and *didn't* cause a stink because he was a man and had the biggest screen hit of the year. Or the singer with the fright wig and the comeback, who was much more fun in the old days when she had a mustache and processed hair, wore ratty fur coats, and sang "Don't Play Me Cheap." Or the other old one who has a hunk manager-husband and wants more money to continue on that nighttime soap opera. Or even the little guy—the one with ants in his pants and too many body-guards—who insulted Liz Taylor. The list goes on and on. You know who they are—overexposed, almost generic faces who have become as predictable as winter's first set of chapped lips.

There's just not enough celebrities to go around. After they've made it to the top, we all know it's downhill from then on. Why bother rooting for them any longer? Look what happened to poor Michael Jackson—no self-respecting thirteen-year-old would be caught dead wearing one glove these days. Once you've become hard news (especially if you make the cover of *Time* or *Newsweek*), who cares? You're no longer delightful to anyone. We must be creative and make up our own celebrities, elevating the obscurely fabulous and turning them into household words in our own communities.

Don't get me wrong. I'm still a fame hag. My head swims every December 31 as I sit by my phone with my own year-end Best and Worst lists neatly printed on file cards. The only problem is, nobody calls. I have no choice but to dial my friends who are trying to celebrate New Year's Eve and bother them with my opinionated announcements: "I know you're in the middle of a party, but do you have ten minutes?" As they roll their eyes and pull up a chair, desperately signaling for a stiff drink, they resign themselves to politely listening. Satisfied that I have their undivided attention, I begin:

Best Movie Title: We have a three-way tie—the winners are the porno takeoffs *Bimbo—Hot Blood, Part II, The Sperminator,* and *Romancing the Bone.* Most Amazing Support Groups: Parents of children who have died from autoerotic suicide (death from masturbation while hanging oneself to heighten the orgasm) and HONEST (Help Our Neighbors Establish Sanity and Truth), formed by accused child molesters (many from the McMartin School in southern California) who say they're innocent. And, of course, Best Animal of the Year: Who else but Twiggy, winner of the Ugly Dog Contest, whose hairless body has warts and sometimes severe acne. Her owner, Patsy Dawson of Paramount, California (I just had to call her), confided that she can't take Twiggy out for walks because people panic. " 'Is it a dog?' people would say. Others would be afraid and yell out, 'Hold it!' when the dog is not more than four pounds —they act like it's a Saint Bernard." Mrs. Dawson, who appeared with Twiggy on *The Johnny Carson Show* and in *People* magazine, admits that fame "was fun in the beginning, but it's gotten kind of nerve-racking. I work a forty-hour week. My mother has taken over handling Twiggy's stardom."

Of course, my choice for *Time's* Man of the Year is none

other than Dr. Steven Rosenberg, the physician who actually saw Ronald Reagan's asshole. Think of the power! Imagine him reeling from privilege, walking on air past network camera crews, going home to his proud wife and announcing, "I saw it, honey. I saw it with my own eyes!" Understandably, Nancy Reagan hated the news coverage of the removal of an "ominously large growth in the president's colon," and White House chief of staff Donald T. Regan was, according to *Newsweek*, "fuming about tasteless drawings of the president's bowels appearing in some newspapers." But White House deputy press secretary Larry Speakes saved the day with, beyond a doubt, the wittiest quip of 1985. When asked whether Reagan would display his scar the way LBJ did after his famous operation, Speakes replied that the president would be more likely to show the media "the point of entry of yesterday's exam." *Touché!* One for the history books.

Sometimes you have to recycle celebrities to make them interesting, and they can be even better the second time around. Case in point: the fabulous and talented Miss Joey Heatherton, star of stage, screen, Vegas, and mattress commercials. Close your eyes and imagine what it would be like to wake up one day and *be* Joey Heatherton. On July 8, 1985, it must not have felt so hot. Joey, goddess, was detained in the U.S. passport office at Rockefeller Center for allegedly becoming abusive at not receiving special treatment in the passport line. Supposedly, she threw a tantrum, grabbed passport-office clerk Mary Polik, tore her hair out, and smashed her head against the Formica counter. Oh, well, nobody's perfect. I rushed to New York for the federal-court hearing and was crushed to find that it had been postponed. If you really idolize a celebrity, you become your own reporter and work hard to spread the fame. I've always wanted to star Joey in one of my productions, but since my budgets never allow for flying in big stars for screen tests, I was hoping for a cut-rate audition right in the courtroom. Instead, I dashed over to the passport office and interviewed the security guard who had detained Joey.

"She was obnoxious first, then violent," he said, showing me the exact counter where the attack allegedly took place. Seeing the long lines snaking around the office, I could imagine how she felt. Did some young whippersnapper embarrass Joey by rudely snarling, *"Who?"* when she announced, *"I am Joey Heatherton"?*

"She [Miss Polik] hasn't been back to work since," the guard continued. "She wears a neck brace and has a $6 million lawsuit against Heatherton. Joey kept repeating, 'I have to go to Paris,' and tried to pay with a $100 bill, but you have to have exact change." Well, no wonder Joey grabbed her, I thought. It costs $42 for a passport, and hundred-dollar bills are hardly rare in New York. As I approached the infamous information window, I tried to imagine reaching my own arm through the small opening in the Plexiglas protection shield and ripping the hair of every low-level bureaucrat who has ever abused his power in the past. Way to go, Joey! Buy her a wig and knock 'em dead in Paris!

Actually, you don't even need real celebrities to make your day; your own friends can be much more exciting. My phone was ringing off the hook from all over the East Coast after another bad mood made the news. A woman I know from my many summers in Provincetown walked into a restaurant in this eccentric beach community and, according to the *Cape Cod Times*, "demanded a drink." When told the lounge wouldn't open until later in the day, she allegedly pulled out a loaded twelve-gauge double-barreled shotgun and threw down a wad of money. She also happened to have with her a "hunting knife" and a "powerful compound bow with three razor-tipped arrows." She was carrying "$7,000 in cash" (think of the tip!) and "100 grams of cocaine." Talk about

Rambo! "Did she have a shopping cart to carry all the weapons?" friends wondered, trying to cut the conversation short so they could rush to photocopy the article while it was still hot. When this rather aggressive customer was finally released on bail from jail, she reappeared at all the local fashionable watering holes, and no one dared mention the incident. "Are you kidding?" commented a friend who had barred her in the past from his restaurant. "She might have a cannon!" Suddenly the whole town had newfound respect for this reluctant newsmaker. And you can be sure she can count on tip-top service in the future. Buy the lady a drink, for God's sake!

You likewise shouldn't worry about missing all the celebrity nightlife that you read about in New York's syndicated gossip columns. Most of the celebrants at Area, Limelight, and the Palladium aren't famous anyway; they just think they are. You can be decadent in your own hometown. Whenever I'm feeling especially wicked in Baltimore, I drop by an after-hours club officially named the Wee Hours but known to aficionados as the Wee-Wee. It's really scary and glamorous. Anybody can get in. Getting *out* is the problem. The "in" crowd is made up of mean, tattooed go-go girls off work, hustlers between tricks, and biker gangs all "as drunk as they can get," according to a local police spokesman, who adds, "It's the last place in Baltimore to get laid."

Socially, it's just like going to jail. Genet would love the mix. I never make eye contact but try to befriend the biggest brute who might protect me should a hostage crisis arise. All sorts of monsters will ask you to dance; if you refuse, they might beat you up. It's a virtual who's who of the streets. There's Big Edna from up Conkling Street—remember all the coverage she got from her PCP ring? And, oh my God, here comes the Pagans biker gang. I thought they all got life for attempted murder of a New Jersey trooper. Maybe we'll be lucky and see them kick some ass tonight. Boy George's birthday bash in New York could never be as exciting as this.

If you just pay attention to your own backyard, you'd realize that scandal is everywhere. If one of your parents is an alcoholic—well, isn't that as exciting as reading about Liza Minnelli? Start spreading the news to all your friends and watch your profile rise in the neighborhood. Is your thirteen-year-old sister an unwed mother? Cheer up, so is Farrah Fawcett, and she doesn't care. Hang a sign on the front of your house posting the number of days left until the birth and update it daily. You watch—people who barely spoke to you before will be falling all over themselves to take her to the hospital.

Nobody has a boring life when you get down to it. Isn't your own existence much more interesting than anyone else's? Look in the mirror and see yourself in a whole different light. It will all happen to you eventually: divorce, complicated operations, addictions of one sort or another, even death. It's lonely at the bottom as well as the top. You're a big celebrity, and you never even realized it. Go tell somebody. *Quickly.*

16

Finally, Footlights on the Fat Girls

The real reason I'm praying that *Hairspray*, the Broadway musical based on my 1988 movie, succeeds is that if it's a hit, there will be high school productions, and finally the fat girl and the drag queen will get the starring parts.

But I'll be honest, I'm a real amateur in the theater world. My experience with the stage is hardly daunting. I still hold it against my parents that they didn't take me to see Tab Hunter and Tallulah Bankhead star in Tennessee Williams' *The Milk Train Doesn't Stop Here Anymore* when it previewed in Baltimore in 1963 (it later died after only five performances on Broadway).

I did grow up obsessed with early Theater of the Absurd (thank you, Grove Press), which led me somehow to the Cockettes' LSD-inspired communist drag queen musicals in San Francisco in the early 1970s. My favorite number in *Gypsy* was "You Gotta Have a Gimmick," and I tried to turn it into a personal spiritual mantra.

Edward Albee was always an idol, and I've seen every one of his plays (including his adaptation of *Lolita*, featuring Shirley Stoler and Carroll Baker's daughter, Blanche). Of course I eagerly attended the revival of Jane Bowles' *In the Summer House* at the Vivian Beaumont Theater in 1993, but even with repeated viewings of the porno video *Oklahomo*, I can't turn myself into a trashy Neil Simon.

Maybe *The Buddy Deane Show*, which inspired *Hairspray*, was the only *wholesome* obsession that ever led to one of my movies. As a kid, I'd fantasize in front of the television every day over the private lives of the Committee members, the teenage regulars who were worshiped or beat up (depending on the neighborhood) when they made personal appearances at record hops to promote the show. I'd imagine all sorts of lurid melodrama in their lives; addiction to cough medicine, cockroaches nesting in the girls' teased hairdos, even stabbings with rat-tail combs.

Long after the show went off the air, I'd boozily try to teach friends after a wild night at the bar how to do the Madison and the other dances I remembered from television. When Buddy Deane finally had a reunion, many decades after the show was canceled, I paid to go like the common groupie I was. Seeing some of my favorite Committee members, now in their forties and still doing the Locomotion without irony, gave me unadulterated pleasure. This led to the "Where Are They Now?" article I wrote about the dancers for *Baltimore* magazine (Chapter 9 in this book), which gave me an excuse to nose around in their personal lives. Later, the Committee gave me an "Honorary Buddy Deane Committee Member" diploma that left me both honored and mortified.

Then I accidentally made a family movie about it all. I remember when the Motion Picture Association of America came back with a PG rating for *Hairspray*. I hung my head in shame. "I'll never work again," I moaned as New Line, the distributor of the film, suggested I add a mild four-letter word to get a PG-13 rating. But I resisted. If we were going to surprise anybody it would be with wholesomeness. "A family movie both the Bradys and the Mansons could adore," David Edelstein wrote in my all-time favorite review of the picture, in *Rolling Stone*. But can crackpot memories be turned into a joyous vehicle *twice*?

Margo Lion, the Broadway producer, seemed to think so. I explained that *Hairspray* the sitcom never got past the pilot stage in the late eighties, and the movie had already been optioned once before for Broadway. But this former Baltimorean (and a stranger to me) explained how she wanted "to keep the John Waters spirit intact" and make it work. My ears perked up. Could I possibly collaborate? Me, the ultimate control freak? It was a scary thought.

As soon as I heard an early version of the *Hairspray* score and lyrics by Marc Shaiman and Scott Wittman, I was hooked. Remembering my childhood obsession with Cyril Ritchard's portrayal of Captain Hook in the Mary Martin *Peter Pan*, I suddenly wanted to be part of a Broadway show again. But imagine how frightened I *really* was, all alone, at the first table reading. Total strangers were turning something I thought up fifteen years ago in the bedroom of my old apartment into a big splashy musical—the kind of contemporary entertainment that usually inspires Hallmark greeting cards and my immediate distrust. Relief poured from my brow as I realized that the book by Mark O'Donnell and Thomas Meehan was taking my screenplay by the sprocket holes, giving it a bon-voyage kiss, and hurling it onstage like a brand-new baby. My jokes were still there and they wanted to sing!

You'd think I'd be the *Hairspray* musical's harshest critic, but I've turned into a cultist, going most nights to the previews in both Seattle and New York, dressed like John Waters. Somehow, I've resisted the urge to yell out the dialogue and dance along like a demented June Taylor Dancer to Jerry Mitchell's blue-collar inspired dance-drunk-in-my-apartment choreography.

My job? Studio executive and *Grease* police. Giving "notes" and being shocked that they were actually wanted. Harping on the fact that the fifties are used up and the early sixties had a very different, rarified look. And as far as Baltimore authenticity—well, I was their man.

No, they didn't have malts in East Baltimore, and the blue-collar lead character, Tracy Turnblad, would definitely *not* want to go to Goucher College. Imagine the thrill (and the nerve) of telling the Tony Award–winning costume designer William Ivey Long that, yes, Van Smith, the costume designer for the film, had it right. Good girls in Baltimore did wear "angel blouses," those mock maternity tops that baited parents' horror of teenage pregnancies. I also had a hairdo "how to" book that the wig icon Paul Huntley used to create some of the most atrocious bouffant "hairdon'ts" seen on a Broadway stage. Even the late Chris Mason, the grouchy and witty hairdresser who did the hairstyling for the movie, would, I hope, nod down her approval from hairdo-heaven.

The director, Jack O'Brien, came to Baltimore searching for inspiration, and when he looked to the gutter with reverence rather than condescension, I knew he was a kindred spirit. I gave him and the rest of the creative team the "John Waters tour," the "hair hopper" dress shops, beauty parlors and formstone row houses that so inspired Vincent Peranio, the production designer of my films. When I later saw David Rockwell's Necco Wafer–colored Baltimore stage design, I had to chuckle remembering the wrong turn we took in my car that day, ending us up in a very scary dead-end street surrounded by festive white-boy crackheads.

I also tried to explain to the writers how nervous I was in 1988 to have an "integration comedy" on my hands. I had been hassled by separatist lesbian groups in 1976 for my *Desperate Living* script ("How dare a *man* make a comedy about lesbians!"), and now I was putting out a movie where the line "I have a dream" was a gag.

The subtle shades of discrimination in my hometown

were something the Broadway crew had to understand. As a child in Baltimore County, I used to lie in bed at night and hear "colored people" walking up to the tiny "Negro community" near our house, singing a cappella the beautiful "race music" that so scared our white parents. By junior high, every cool white kid I knew listened to all-black radio (WSID, WEBB, WWIN), but very few had black friends. At white record hops, black singers could lip-sync their rhythm-and-blues hits but never dance with whites *or* with each other. You could really get shunned by whites *and* blacks for mixing the races socially. I even got beat up outside an *art* school in Baltimore for bringing a black girl as my date. And black cops would really hassle our racially mixed crowd, stopping our car for no reason and growling, "This isn't Greenwich Village, you know." I knew.

As a film director, I realized on the first day of rehearsal that a Broadway show is one big master shot; no coverage, no retakes, no looping—just endlessly precise rehearsals and daily rewrites. Casting, for me, was like entering *The Twilight Zone*. I had seen Harvey Fierstein out of costume, playing the part that the late Divine made famous in the movie, and was thrilled at Harvey's original un-drag-queen-like take on the role: Tom Waits meets Dagmar meets Miss Frances from *Ding Dong School*. But seeing him getting into drag for the first time really gave me the willies. No matter how different two actors are in real life, two "ample" men half in drag look the same. It was like having an LSD flashback. All I could think was that from beyond the grave, Divine would have been proud. Alive, he'd want the part.

And Marissa Jaret Winokur as Tracy Turnblad, well, seeing her singing her heart out in that tight blue skirt and ruffled blouse as the curtain rises, I can only remember the same excitement my longtime casting director Pat Moran and I felt the first day Ricki Lake arrived on the set of the film.

I'm astounded and proud that the characters we brought to the screen have been so faithfully transformed onto the stage for the next generation of *Hairspray* chubby-chaser enthusiasts.

Who knows? Maybe I can get all my old films working again. Marc Shaiman and Scott Wittman could definitely write a great off-Broadway score for *Female Trouble;* Marissa could play Divine's role as a teenager and Harvey could take over for the adult part. Just think of the final number as she gets the electric chair—"I Want to Live *and* Eat!" *Multiple Maniacs* could be a game show, *Pink Flamingos* an opera, *Desperate Living* a sitcom, *Polyester* an ice show, *Serial Mom* a video game, *Pecker* a video installation, and *Cecil B. DeMented* a reality TV show.

And, hey, even *Hairspray* the Broadway musical could be a new Hollywood movie, and then the porno world could do the knockoff—*Hair-pie*—coming soon to adult video.

17

Catty Corner

Here's what's been getting on my nerves in the last twenty-four hours:

1) Charities that junk-mail you those cheesy personal home-address labels that criminals love to find in your garbage can to use in mail-fraud scams.
2) Magazines that try to trick you into "early renewal" by mailing out misleading subscription bills that aren't really due for six to eight months.
3) CD packaging that is designed to infuriate the buyer. Can anyone open a new CD without ripping the labeling tape unevenly, breaking the box, or using one of those plastic utensils that should never be needed in the first place?
4) The term "creative black tie," which usually encourages people who know better to dress stupidly.
5) East Coast white people who overcelebrate the first day of springlike weather by leaving the house practically naked. That night, when the sun has gone down and the temperature has plunged, I secretly chuckle as they stand shivering at the bus stop trying to get home.
6) Guests who respond to your dinner invitation with "I'd love to attend but you know I have diet restrictions." No, I didn't. "You might want to eat before you come," I snarl. Didn't your mother ever tell you "If you don't like

the food, mess up your plate a little and the host will think you ate what was served"?

7) Friends who RSVP my Christmas party invitation for two who ask "Can I bring a third person? We're having company from out of town, blah, blah, blah." "No, you can't and now *you're* not invited" is my policy and believe me, it works.

8) Overly fashion-enthused salespeople in fancy clothing stores who won't leave you alone to shop for yourself even after you've politely said "just looking" five times. "Here's something I *really* like," they continue to gush. A stern "I wasn't thinking of buying *you* a present" usually does the trick.

9) Telephone solicitors. "What do you have on?" I pant lewdly to them and they never call back.

10) I hate myself for this one, but I can't help resenting airlines that open up the first-class lavatories to coach passengers who wait in line next to my overpriced seat, farting their way to Europe.

18

Crimes of Fashion: A Look Inside
the Criminal Wardrobe

I don't judge criminals by the terrible crimes they commit, I judge them by what they wear. Sometimes I forgive them if they dress well for court, and I'm almost always for parole if they've used fashion in a creative way while serving time behind bars. Fashion can be a crime if it's done right.

Of course, there can also be criminal fashion disasters. Not every convict can be as effortlessly ravishing as, say, Richard "Night Stalker" Ramirez can be with a pair of sunglasses. John Wayne Gacy is without a doubt the worst-dressed mass murderer in America, followed closely by Richard Speck and Juan Corona. Look what a leather jacket did for Claus von Bülow. Imelda Marcos may have had thousands of pairs of shoes, but each and every pair was common. Zsa Zsa, of course, should have been sentenced to pick up trash along the freeway, dressed in the same hideous outfits she wore to court.

To fully understand criminal chic, one must study the crime scene. Even the least fashion-conscious homicide detective could deduce that Jean Harris and Ted Bundy had the same preppy designer influences. Cheryl Crane, Lana Turner's daughter, was lucky enough to have an alert, style-conscious grandmother on duty that fateful Good Friday in

1958 when Cheryl came to Lana's rescue and stabbed lowlife monster and girlfriend-beater Johnny Stompanato to death. Her grandmother, Cheryl remembers, "sensed that the bloodied, handmade lacy pink peignoir, by Jules Parks, of course," would be all wrong for photo ops. Cheryl quickly changed into a "good-girl kelly green skirt, sweater, flat black shoes, polo coat, and white silk head scarf" to stylishly heighten her innocence. Though she may have privately favored a "pair of jeans and a black leather motorcycle jacket," the coroner's jury hadn't a clue, and the verdict of justifiable homicide set her free for a life of fashion confidence, reflected today in her stunning Donna Karan and Armani wardrobe.

Charles Schmid, Jr., the "Pied Piper of Tucson," wasn't so lucky. Famed not so much for his mid-sixties killing of three teenage girls as for his mind-boggling fashion statements, he was sentenced to death, one suspects, for his atrocious taste. "Smitty," as he was called, pompadoured his dyed, jet-black hair and wore a thick coat of pancake over his dirty, unshaven, handsome face. His Casanova lips were covered in white lipstick, and he designed a quarter-size beauty mark made of putty that resembled a hideous cartoon witch's mole. His ultimate accessory was the large, filthy bandage he wore on his nose for no apparent reason. Like all models, he wished he were taller, so he stuffed his boots with a three-inch layer of tin cans and rags. Dressing conservatively for his trial didn't seem to fool anybody. Smitty's death sentence was later commuted to life, and except for a brief escape in 1972, he was a model prisoner until murdered by fellow inmates in 1975. Charles Schmid, Jr., had received his final fashion review.

His mentor in style may have been Charles Starkweather, the first mass murderer/pinup boy—a Bruce Weber model way before his time. Caril Fugate, the fourteen-year-old who accompanied him (many believe as an innocent hostage) on a two-day homicide spree that claimed ten lives (three of which were in Caril's family), became the youngest female tried for murder in America. They were fashion pioneers (the movie *Badlands* is based on them) who shocked the nation and virtually cemented the cool juvenile-delinquent look first introduced by James Dean in the mid-fifties. The press photographers ate them alive. Charles gave good sneer and made young girls' hormones go into spasms as he was televised bloodied in chains, wearing tight black denim pants (the real kind—the ones they don't make anymore), a black leather motorcycle jacket, white cowboy boots, and a cigarette dangling from his lips.

Caril, on the other hand, was so tiny, so young, and so hard as she sipped a Pepsi in the police car after her arrest that she may have scared America even more than Charlie. Probably terrified, but looking defiant, she set the tone for bad-girl fashion for decades to come: black slacks, an oversize light blue (her favorite color) men's coat, drum-majorette boots, and a scarf tied coal-miner-widow-style around the one detail that might have saved her—a good-girl ponytail that the world would never see.

The world did, however, sit bolt upright in shock when it saw the most notorious hairdo from hell in crime history, which still keeps "Moors Murderess" Myra Hindley firmly behind English prison bars. Forget that she and her boyfriend, Ian Brady, kidnapped and murdered children in 1966 so they could tape-record their screams for later entertainment—it was the hairdo that people could never forgive.

At age fifteen, Myra first gave herself a homemade-bleach job. Peroxide apparently gave her a thrill like no other, and she escalated to a full-color stripping with no toner at a local beauty salon (forever blackened in beauty history), Maison Laurette. Color-chart abuse ran rampant until finally Myra's evil coif reached its criminal peak, tinted a daring pink. Unfortunately, when she was finally arrested, Myra's dark roots were showing in all their hideous glory. The mug shot taken that day—the one that has graced the cover of countless true-crime paperbacks—will forever reflect those few foolish days she so unwisely procrastinated proper beauty maintenance.

Sometimes just being tried for murder can perk up a person's fashion sense. When John Linley Frazier executed the entire Santa Cruz family of Dr. Vincent Ohta in 1970 dressed in nondescript trousers, an off-the-rack green coat, hideous ankle-high Hiawatha moccasins, and a straw hat with a red-white-and-blue headband, the arresting officer, Deputy Sheriff Rodney Sanford, apparently resisted the urge to stick a feather in Frazier's hat and call him Macaroni. Who in the international fashion press could have predicted the incredible flair and sartorial splendor this defendant would show on the first day of his sanity hearing? Maybe courtrooms *are* the ultimate runways, for Mr. Frazier had been busy in his holding tank, shaving bald the left side of his hair, beard, mustache, and eyebrows. The right side of his face was still covered in a luxuriant growth of hair. If this boy had been given a scholarship to FIT, would he have killed?

Gertrude Baniszewski didn't have a lot of time for fashion. She was too busy defending herself in an Indiana courtroom in 1966 against the charges that she and her children had tortured and murdered a foster child after carving "I am a prostitute and proud of it" on her chest. Before all this trouble, she hadn't been that particular about what she wore—white-trash flip-flops and cheap housedresses with a pocket for her Kools were A-OK with her. All that ironing she took in for money to feed her family made her hate the sight of a new outfit; cotton was her enemy. Now that the jury was gawking, she wore the cardigan sweaters and pleated skirts provided by her lawyers, but it didn't do any good. She got life anyway.

Twenty long years later, Mrs. Baniszewski walked out of prison on parole, fashion-rehabilitated at last. Clutching a woven envelope bag full of job opportunities, she looked confident of her future in a London Fog all-weather coat over a light brown, dressed-for-success suit worn with a crocheted blue muffler that represented the debt she had paid to society. Her rigidly sprayed and dyed artichoke hairdo symbolized control over her own life, and her autumn-hued, stenciled eyebrows and shocking-pink lipstick cried out for leniency. Her sedate pearl earrings whispered, "I'm sorry." Fashion society was about to give Gertrude another chance.

Having an insanely eccentric attorney can also enhance your chances in court. The patron saint of "crime hags" has to be Gladys Towler Root, called by her biographer Cy Rice "Defender of the Damned." A specialist in defending and winning sex cases in the late fifties in Los Angeles, her clients were child molesters, rapists, and peeping toms. Her main weapon in court was fashion. Tourists lined up outside her courtrooms to gawk at her insane drag-queen-like costumes. Would she wear the full-length lavender robe with her hair dyed Mercurochrome purple to match? Or the black lace number with the multicolored sequins and pink ostrich plumes? So abominable were her outfits that juries usually acquitted her clients, apparently reasoning that their crimes were nothing compared with Ms. Root's fashion atrocities. If there were an electric chair for fashion blunders, Gladys Towler Root would have fried the day she passed the bar.

I'm against the death penalty, of course, but it does lend a certain gravity to shopping. "Is my dress pulled down?" were the last words whispered by Bonnie Hedy to her codefendant, Carl Hall, as they were strapped into matching his-and-hers seats in the Missouri gas chamber for the 1953 kidnapping-murder of six-year-old Bobby Greenleigh. And pushing the "You can never be too thin" maxim to the limit, "Little" Eva Coo—hair, makeup, and nails done perfectly—refused her last meal in Sing-Sing before her 1934 electrocution with the ultimate in throwaway wit. "I don't want to eat; it's bad for my figure," she told matrons. "Besides, I'm on a diet."

Thinking of committing a crime? Please remember when planning your offense that it takes only a few seconds longer to look stylish. Pore over this season's collections and decide which haute couture criminal look screams "You!"

Want to start small? Chanel's quilted-velvet vertical clutch bag seems perfect for shoplifting, and Versace's voluminous orange flared evening coat with a dramatic shawl collar can camouflage even larger thefts, such as TVs or chain saws. Katharine Hamnett's quilted hot pants under her snappy fitted jacket with zipper front and slash pockets are de rigueur for cat-burglaring and have the freedom of movement you'll need if you have to run from the cops. Thierry Mugler knows that silly little fingerprints can be a nuisance, so he designed a stunning pair of gold-lamé men's driving gloves to eradicate this problem. And if you want to go big-time with a capital offense, eliminate all witnesses with Christian Lacroix's beautifully alluring green midriff-length tissue-taffeta scarf that strangles with subtle aplomb.

The courtroom is, of course, center stage, and each member of the jury is your own personal John Fairchild. If you are some kind of crazy militant, I'd suggest Issey Miyake's storm-trooper suit—very terrorist, very now. Insanity pleas take special planning, but the extra expense is usually worth the effort. This year I'd go with Gaultier's jeweled Napoleon hat with hanging silk-knotted tassels worn over his Jackson Pollock–inspired, paint-splattered suit. And perjured crocodile tears flow beautifully through Comme des Garçons irregular and rumpled handkerchiefs that magically appear vintage as you whip them out of your pocketbook.

My first choice to design for the firing squad would be Thierry Mugler, whose black leather sleeveless mock-turtleneck muscle T-shirt would have looked positively dreamy on Gary Gilmore. Issey Miyake's startling combination court jester/executioner hat can only enhance your struggling in the gas chamber when you pull it down over your nostrils to get a few bonus seconds of modeling time before suffocating in front of the notoriously squeamish fashion press. And for the ultimate in fashion epiphanies, pray, just pray, that the electrodes are double-strength when you are strapped into that hot seat of style, dressed in your drop-dead Versace metallic ensemble with the electrifying fringe that, combined with your own internal voltage, explodes in one beautiful, terrible second, launching you past Diana Vreeland, past Babe Paley, past fashion heaven into your rightful place in the next stratosphere of criminal history.

19

Independent Spirit Awards 2001

Welcome to the Sixteenth Annual IFP/West Independent Spirit Awards. Sort of like the Betty Ford Clinic with drinks, isn't it? It's nice to be invited back—you can never have too many careers. I feel like a combination of Allan Carr and a Dick-Clark-Who-Ages. I think the real reason they asked me to be host is that I'm the only name they could find who *isn't* nominated for something today. But being a loser is OK; it's "edgy" and that's what we're here to celebrate. Everybody wants to be "edgy" these days. I'm on the board of the Provincetown Film Festival, and every year we give out a "Filmmaker on the Edge" award. The coolest theaters claim only to book "edgy" films and the independent distributors brag that they alone know how to market a film with "edge." Even the Spirit Awards has been called "the edgiest award show on TV," and we're gonna try and live up to that today. Hey, I subscribe to 118 magazines a month and there're films nominated today that *I've* never heard of! We're off to a good start.

Since I am the host, I can't resist giving the producers ideas on how to make the show more memorable next year, even though I know many of the ideas are not cinematically correct.

I think we should send all the picked-through gift baskets

left behind today to the homes of the Spirit Award nominees who didn't show up today—especially if they're you-know-where tomorrow night.

All the presenters should announce their addictions as they come on stage. "Hi, I'm John Waters, and I'm the Robert Downey, Jr., of cigarettes"—which is true, and I'm proud to share with you tonight! You can't blackmail a celebrity who admits everything. If movie stars spilled the dirt on themselves *first*, the tabloids wouldn't be here today taking photos that they'll later use to illustrate phony stories about your next marital breakup.

Let's be honest and admit that everybody here today encourages teenagers to see R-rated films. The future winners of the Independent Spirit Awards are sneaking into R-rated movies as I speak. What teenager who wants to be in showbiz accepts a restricted rating? One who will *never* make a film, that's who!

Since the Golden Globes serve liquor and the TV critics always bring this up favorably for "loosening up the show," I propose next year giving out bongs. Imagine movie-star bad trips; anorexia meets the munchies! And maybe Harrison Ford will come!

Hire somebody for hosting next year whom you know will lose it on stage. Don't you think Elizabeth Taylor secretly copied Ally Sheedy's persona from the Spirit Awards a few years back? I do, and they both were great moments in television.

Steal promotional ideas from foreign journalists. *The Sun*, London's most rabid tabloid newspaper, has a dog named Charlie that is trained to smell cocaine. Charlie is taken to every movie premiere and lunges at celebrities on the red carpet who are "holding" drugs—imagine the excitement of movie stars running preshow to their limos with Charlie barking in hot pursuit.

Now some "edge" advice for all the stars here today; not washing your hair is not enough anymore. You've got to keep reinventing your image to attract a younger, angrier generation of obsessive film directors.

If you're known for being "really sweet," become a monster for the day. Going against type is always a good career move, and you'll get more coverage. Surprise the press on the red carpet by announcing in a humorless voice to anyone who'll listen "I'm more independent than these sellouts! *Nobody* saw my last film, and I'm proud of it!"

Bring an alarming date. If you're part of a famous movie-star couple, swap partners and arrive at different times. The photographers will go wild. If you're gay and trying to hide it, bring Anna Nicole Smith to confuse the issue. Every year I invite Don Knotts to be my date—hey, we all have a type—and every year his people politely decline. "Write a part for Don!" his agent told me this year but I don't have the nerve to tell him "I use the casting couch!"

Let's talk about fashion. Movie stars, you cheap bastards, pay for your outfits! You can afford them! Free clothes are for the poor, not actors. Donate the money your free outfit you're wearing today costs to the homeless. Or better yet—the "fashionless"—a new "trendy" minority waiting to happen.

Be nice to your "independent" fans—believe me, they haven't been waiting for three days in bleachers out front to get your autograph, they're home designing insane websites about your private life. One night I went out in Baltimore to a bar and the next morning on the Web was a report that I went to the men's room in the bar, took a leak, didn't wash my hands, and later shook hands with fans. Now there's a fan who cares! Be nice to these lunatics. They usually turn into journalists.

And now for some advice for today's nominees.

Be a bad loser—nobody ever is. Sob uncontrollably when the other name is announced; the cameras might stay on you instead. Rush into the press tent and give your planned acceptance speech even though you lost. Better yet, steal the winner's wallet while he or she's on stage. Believe me, winners never "watch their bag" in moments of glory.

And if you *are* a winner, let's get one thing out of the way—none of this "I was in the bathroom" when your name is called. One would think a serious nominee would eliminate *before* coming to an awards show!

Being a bad winner is even edgier than being a bad loser. Thank nobody on stage. Whip out your prepared speech on expensive monogrammed stationery and read the three words you've written, "I deserved it." Recite from memory the two negative reviews you got on the picture and name the critics who wrote them.

Leave immediately after your acceptance speech, not caring about the awards that come after yours.

The next day, release a statement to the press with your opinions on who came in second, third, and fourth place. Make special fun of who you think came in fifth.

Finally—try to pick up somebody today. Does anybody get lucky at awards shows? Do the winners ever go home with a loser's date? Do people get laid at the IFP Awards? I need to know. Look around you—show business people have loose morals. All award shows are too long. Get busy—you've got the time. This is Hollywood!

PART II

I'm back because the screenplay award is coming up next. I guess I'm qualified to introduce the nominees, since one critic wrote that my plots "were merely the clothesline to hang out my dirty wash." All writers have their clotheslines and we're all looking for that next load of wash—clean or dirty. "Oh, God," we wonder, "what can we write that nobody else has written?" A Sing-A-Long Dogma tragedy? A remake of *Ice Castles?* An all-nude PG-13 *Rapunzel* for hyperactive children? A postmodern Meryl Streep splatter film?

Whenever I start a script, I know it's time to get in my car and drive around Baltimore snooping and spying. Inspiration comes from exaggerating real life. I always do the location scout first before I even begin to write the narrative. I pick the neighborhood where the characters live, choose their actual homes, and watch the neighbors doing yard work, shopping for groceries, taking out the garbage, and then fantasize about all the horrible and hopefully funny things that could happen in their lives.

Since my new script is about blue-collar sex addicts and their search for some kind of dignity, I've decided it's unwise to talk to the neighbors about the script this early in the process. Most of the time I stay in my plain narcotics-agent type of car anyway, writing notes and imagining all sorts of hideous scenes to take place in their living rooms. But sometimes they see me and mistake me for a snoopy insurance adjuster or worse yet, a flasher. I peel out with my ideas and hope they don't remember me when the real location scout knocks on their door months later.

Eavesdropping has always been an important source material for dialogue. Just open your ears and pretend you're not listening, and you'll be amazed at the lunatic things people actually say. In a fancy restaurant in Baltimore I heard the waiter ask a woman patron if she'd like dessert. "Christ, no—I'm bloated," she classily answered. And in a local supermarket I saw this beautiful angelic child wander momentarily away from her mother. "Get over here, you little shit-ass!" Mom growled, damaging the child's self-esteem but giving me some sparkling new dialogue.

Let's talk about this NC-17 rating! Isn't it time writers band together to rehabilitate the ridiculous stigma of this supposed "adult" rating? A European intellectual who had just arrived in America told me he could barely speak English when he saw a movie theater marquee that read "two adult hits" and went inside expecting intelligent, well-written, thought-provoking American movies. That's what an NC-17 rating *should* mean.

Face it, there's only one taboo left in movies, and that's why the MPAA is in business—to stop Hollywood A-List stars from having real sex on film with Screen Actors Guild–approved penetration. It's already happening in Europe, and it will happen in the United States within the next decade! I guarantee it! But movie stars, we need your help; writers can think it up, but you have to do it! Once the star legitimizes "reality sex," there will be nothing left for the MPAA to fear, and the curse of NC-17 will be meaningless. Have courage—critics and the American public will accept you in taboo-breaking material as long as it's done in a clever, ironic way.

I salute whomever takes this chance! Who will it be? (*looking into audience*)

How about you, Chloë Sevigny?* Come on, Meg Tilly, go down in film history. Let the Golden Age of Censor-Free Independent film begin. Think of the new "edge" you'll acquire when you casually mention to the press, "If done tastefully, with a good script and a visionary director, I have no problem with penetration." Just think, you might even win the Independent Spirit Award.

---

*Apparently, she took my advice. In the much-maligned *The Brown Bunny* (2003), she gives Vincent Gallo on-screen oral sex.

20

John Waters Presents: *Boom!*

I never rewatch the great films of my favorite directors because I'm afraid they won't hold up. But there is one movie (and no one has *ever* called it great) that I still watch over and over again. As a matter of fact, I use it as a sort of "test screening" of new friends—if they don't respond favorably, well . . . we won't meet again. It's called *Boom!*, the ridiculously retitled film version of the Tennessee Williams play *The Milk Train Doesn't Stop Here Anymore*. Directed by Joseph Losey in 1968, and with a screenplay by Tennessee himself, *Boom!* is beyond bad, the other side of camp—a film so genuinely beautiful and awful that there is only one word to describe it: perfect.

Taylor, in the ultimate drag queen role, plays Sissy Goforth, a fabulously rich, self-involved, imperialistic lunatic who has retired to an amazingly art-directed L.A.-style summer home in Sardinia to write her blowhard memoirs and die of some mysterious disease. Parading around in couture outfits credited to "Tiziani of Rome" and ranting to her servants "I have complete domain on this island!" Miss Goforth confides to her secretary, "I need myself a lover." Enter Burton, the "Angel of Death," who "has the unfortunate reputation of calling on a lady a step before the undertaker." Dressed in a Japanese warrior outfit provided by his hostess, Burton is forever looking to the crashing surf below the cliffs of Miss

Goforth's love nest and intoning with a straight face, "Boom! The sound of each moment, of still being alive!" I always rewind my badly duped pirate video to this line and play it over and over until I have reached a kind of Tennessee Williams–inspired druglike trance.

Favorite scene: Goforth invites her catty neighbor, "The Witch of Capri," to lunch. Played by Noël Coward (Katharine Hepburn turned down the role, insulted to have been asked), the Witch makes his entrance being carried off the boat by his male servant. "Yooo-hooo, Sissy!" he cries out in some bizarre ritual of greeting. "Yooo-hooo," she cries back, dressed in an eye-popping jeweled Kabuki outfit that gives new meaning to the word "overdressed." "Is it true you had all those monkey-gland shots in Switzerland?" asks Goforth over a lunch of boiled "sea monster" before being stricken with Camille-like coughing attacks and being put to bed by her servants as she screams for her "injections!" "You're just wrought up, dear," says the Witch as he drunkenly stumbles down to Burton's bed and passes out. Boom.

Everybody hated *Boom!*—the critics, the public, and especially Taylor-Burton fans, who were totally bewildered. Losey has said in print that he was the first director "ever to make a picture with the Burtons that lost money." *Boom!* is never revived in movie theaters and has yet to have a DVD release. But I've always loved it, and I'll shout it from the rooftops. Tennessee Williams was right when he wrote in his *Memoirs*, "I feel that *Boom!* was an artistic success and that eventually it will be received with acclaim."

I hope I've started the ball rolling. Boom!

21

Independent Spirit Awards 2002

PART I

Welcome to the Seventeenth Annual IFP/West Independent Spirit Awards. The awards show that seems to believe David Lynch is too commercial this year. Where a feel-good movie about a child molester with a hard-on of gold wins the most nominations. An award show that celebrates what will come in sixth at the Oscars. And to top it off, you have me, a mentally ill host who wishes someone *would* streak him tonight, a host who encourages winners' long-winded political speeches about causes we've *never* heard of so viewers can laugh derisively at the self-importance of showbiz blowhards.

We've had a tough year. Independent film struggles at the box office. Did you know, some nights, in some theaters, not even one person comes to see our films when they're playing? You think I'm kidding, but I'm not. Check the local details of your box-office reports. It's no misprint. A lonely Monday at the 10 P.M. show somewhere in mid-America, every seat is empty. You've done the press junket, you've gained all that weight for the role, you've worked for scale to prove how serious you are about your craft, and still not one single solitary person cares. No one came. And the theater employees are actually *happy*—they get to go home early with full pay.

Even when times are bad, we're still lucky to be in show business. Suppose the unspeakable happened and suddenly you were a normal person, a "civilian" as they say out here in Hollywood. Stars, remember the few times you *weren't* recognized in a store and how shabbily you were treated? This is normal life for most Americans. No celebrity, no power, no free food, and worse yet, no gift bags! Suppose you had to spend your own money. Imagine being invited to a party and you have to bring the host a present instead of the other way around!? And two-week paid vacations like most people? You've got to be kidding! Hollywood's closed for a month just at Christmas and everybody's Jewish! At least the paparazzi would leave you alone but then you realize the only photos taken of you would be at family get-togethers and the pictures wouldn't be retouched! Being recognized can be humbling even in the best of times. A flight attendant on a plane recently was fussing over me, giving me that celebrity treatment, and just before the flight landed she leaned down and whispered to me happily, "You *are* Ed Wood, aren't you?" She wasn't kidding.

I advise you all to have back-up careers, just in case. I do; I have a vaudeville act, I just played a pedophile priest in *Blood Feast II*, and if I had to I could be a teacher in jail again. Somedays I miss Death Row. I guess even big-time directors are technically eligible for unemployment benefits but it's a little embarrassing if you're recognizable. And besides, they might get you a *real* job. What could any of us do if we couldn't make movies? Directors are always telling people what to do in films, but in the workplace we might get punched in the mouth. Where would control freaks like us get work? In a Wal-Mart as a supervisor? Studio heads would make good welfare workers, greenlighting food stamps and emergency vouchers, but power without fame can sometimes be so pitiful.

Think of your worst moment in show business. The morning your film opens and every review that comes through your fax machine trashes your performance. Remember that first day on the set as a director when you called "Action" and the entire crew gave you the finger? Distributors—that awful phone call from the big theater chain advising you that your picture was yanked off every screen after the first matinee due to hostile audience reaction. And what agent can forget his top client O-D-ing at the premiere?

Embrace your failures. Blow up all your negative reviews and post them outside your house. Brag that your film has been rejected by every major international film festival. Publicize the fact that your movie broke the record for the lowest per-screen average. Find out the names of all 105 people who saw your film nationally and send each and every one a personal thank-you note.

If you want to leave the business forever, go insane and have fun. Second ADs—alter the callsheets behind the bossy ADs back and get him fired. DPs—light those divas from below. Give them double chins and bags that even Botox can't disguise. Accountants—actually pay people net point profits. Publicists—if you're handling a star that gets on your nerves, "swag" the bastard—that's what I hear it's called. At the end of your hellish press day, you rush back into the hotel suite just after the star leaves, empty the minibar, steal the liquor, break some of the furniture, stain the sheets with chocolates, and get out quickly. The studio will fume at the hotel's padded bill, the gossip about the star's alcoholism will begin, his or her sex life will be besmirched by the maids, and the offending "talent" will never be the wiser. Movie stars—if you really want to burn some bridges, right after principal photography has been completed on your highbrow project, immediately star in the porno knockoff version—*Hedwig and His Ten Inches*, *Up in My Deep End*, *In the Bedroom Nude*, *Things in My Son's Behind*, and *L.I.E. . . . Down.*

If you change your mind you can always make a comeback. If one of your old films is playing in a revival house, do what an actor of mine did. Since he played the man with the singing sphincter muscle in *Pink Flamingos*, nobody much remembered his face. He'd sit in the audience and when his part came on screen, he'd tap the person sitting next to him on the arm and say, "That's me." Imagine the horror! The word of mouth! What better way to announce "You're back"? If you've always been typecast, switch your image. If Dolly Parton would get out of drag, take off her makeup, and play an alcoholic, she'd win every award there is. Surprise the public. Sissy Spacek—get exaggerated collagen lips! Steve Buscemi—be "too tan" for a year! John Cameron Mitchell—marry a woman!

You know what, maybe it's time for normal people to pull a switch on us and start acting like celebrities themselves. (*looking into camera*) Viewers, do it tomorrow! Give attitude, be privileged, become a star for just one day. Hand out call-sheets to your family that morning scheduling every second of their day with chores to make you look better. Pretend the PTA meeting or the Rotary Club is your own personal premiere. Charge an expensive outfit at your local department store and return it the next day with makeup stains and get your money back. Have a neighbor drive you in their beat-up car, sit in the backseat, and wave to startled passersby. Demand that your partner walk three steps behind you as you enter and remind him or her that you use the casting couch. Carry a cheap pocket tape-recorder, pick your favorite soundtrack cue, and blare the music every time you make a point in the conversation. When friends rush out to greet you, tell them you'd prefer it if they didn't make eye contact. Steal a pocketbook and pretend you thought it was a gift bag. If anyone criticizes your behavior as boorish, sniff that you've always been "review-proof" and then just laugh at how ridiculous celebrity can be.

We all need to laugh at ourselves. If we can think of the most embarrassing failure we've ever had in show business and chuckle, we'll be the strongest survivors of all; proud to be between pictures, proud to be outside the Hollywood system—and honored to be a part of independent film!

PART II

I'm back because there's something else cinematically alarming I feel compelled to share with you. We're here today to honor movies, but if we're really honest, we'll admit most people end up seeing our work on video or DVD. These days, small towns sometimes have only one movie theater left, and I guarantee you *Lumumba* ain't gonna be playing. So they'll see our movies on tape, which is OK. Without video, my early filthy films could never have infected such a motley group of young malcontents. A few kids in the sticks still remember me as their first bad influence, and I can only thank the video business.

DVDs are even better. Leave it to Hollywood to figure out a way to get people to buy the same film *three* times; laser disc, VHS, and now DVD, the technology that inspired the collector gene in all serious movie-lovers. DVDs are now the new hardback books. If you go home with somebody, the first thing you do is snoop through their DVD collection to see if you'll sleep with them. People with bad titles don't get laid. And video only?! Not even a good-night kiss.

DVD buyers seem to demand "bonus footage." Suppose you don't have any left over from your film? Do you have to do reshoots to supply fake outtakes? Buy edited "lifts" that were cut out of other movies with the same stars and pretend they're yours? Hire look-alikes to shoot blooper reels?

And why is it that directors are the only commentators on most DVDs? Isn't it getting a little clichéd? Why not use the editor's voice? "Can't this hack of a director match a shot? You should have seen the footage I had to work with. I *saved* this film." How about the craft service people? We never get to hear from them. Imagine what they'd have to say. "To hell with food issues! That asshole isn't allergic to salt—I put some in her lunch yesterday, and she didn't die, did she? Eat what you're served, ingrate!"

Since the DVD release is getting so important to a film's eventual long-term reputation, isn't it time to make the in-store signings more glamorous? I sign everything the fans bring: birth certificates, school detention slips, parole cards, even a colostomy bag as it pulsated on a customer. Hey, he paid his $29.95 for the DVD—who am I to judge?

I do have a problem with porn on DVD. You can't fast-forward properly—it jumps ahead, missing details. But the porn business knows how to promote, and maybe we ought to pay attention. Take porn-stud Jeff Stryker's example. After appearing totally nude on stage in his play, he would stand naked and fully aroused at the exit while ticket-buyers filed by and had their picture taken with him. Now *that's* what I call showmanship! Hollywood stars could really do the same thing. If you appeared seminude in your film, couldn't you appear seminude in the video store? Oh, come on, you're seminude here today! Face it, our business is based on voyeurism. Even in your best-reviewed motion picture, someone in the audience is imagining you naked. So show it. Show it *raw!* In this business, you've got to be an exhibitionist to survive.

22

Stalker

I'm not a violent person. Really I'm not. I'm just taking a bike ride to the store to buy Jujyfruits, paper towels, and a bottle of Evian on a slightly warm day. Then I see her. A perfect stranger. Maybe a nice person for all I know. But she's wearing the worst outfit known to man: miniskirt with cowboy boots, tube top barely covered by a jacket with fringe hanging all over, and with the kind of hair that used to be called a "Farrah Fawcett."

Live and let live, I think as I pedal harder. I'm a liberal on most things—pro-choice, pro–gay rights, even anti–death penalty—but I admit I can be a Fascist when it comes to fashion. I don't even blame Farrah. You can tell by the latter-day Angel's new messy coiffure that she's mortified to be linked with a hairdo that has been mutating over the last three decades. *But I can't forgive everybody, can I?*

I ride my bike faster—even more annoyed, as I have to stand and pedal to get uphill. I can't stop thinking of this woman's unfortunate outfit. Miniskirts alone are great. Cowboy boots are OK if tucked under pants (over pants is a whole different story). But worn together, they're the sign of a hard-core *hair-hopper* (a fashion victim who spends too much time on his or her "look," does it poorly, and sees no irony in the predicament). Of course, wearing a tube top in the dead of winter is always a fashion crime. Just because you go to the gym doesn't mean the world wants to see your nude body. Try going to the library . . . then I'd like to see you naked.

Calm down, I tell myself, having pedaled into a sweat. But it's too late. The hideous turquoise belt buckle she was wearing flashes through my mind like a traumatic recovered memory, and I snap. *Belt abuse!* That's what I call it. And belt abuse cannot go unpunished!

I do a U-turn, almost get hit by a car driven by a lady in sunglasses with the designer name printed so big I can read it from here ("I'll get you later"), and race downhill so fast my thin, damaged hair actually blows in the breeze.

"Hey, you!" I scream, leaping off my vehicle with the bicycle lock opened like a pair of gleaming handcuffs.

"What the hell?" she stammers, momentarily distracted from God-knows-what illegal fashion fantasies—fur coats worn before Thanksgiving, or suede shoes after Easter?

"You can't wear that," I say, circling her like a lion tamer in the ring.

"Get away, creep," she snarls, ready to hit me with her oversize knockoff Louis Vuitton purse. I lunge and in a split-second lock her left ankle to the leg of the mailbox on the corner as she lets out a scream that could wake the dead.

"Get off her!" yells a man in a car stopped at a red light. As he leaps out, I notice he's wearing a jogging suit. *And I bet he has no plans to jog!* He's probably on his way to the airport to commit the ultimate fashion felony—flying on an airplane dressed in exercise clothes. Now this man—like most others—could easily beat me up, but when he notices my face twisted by fashion dementia (like Don Knotts meets Jeffrey Dahmer), he changes his mind, ducks back in his car, and aims it straight at me. "You're badly dressed!" I scream and jump out of the way in the nick of time.

I cut across the lawn of a garden apartment just as a thirty-something couple are stepping out, dressed in expensive seventies revival clothes. He's even wearing platform shoes. "You can't be dazed and confused at your age," I bark as their ferocious dog charges me. "If you're old enough to remember the fashion, you're too old to wear it again," I manage to yell as I climb over the fence and run.

Police sirens wail in the distance, but I'm too far gone to care. Rushing into the supermarket, I see an elderly woman who looks incredibly surprised. Then I realize it's just her new face-lift. I march right over. "Excuse me, ma'am, but it's quite obvious you've just had cosmetic surgery, and I'm curious. Why in the autumn of your years would you not choose a look of confidence or dignity instead of the stunned surprise of a deer caught in the headlights of a Mack truck?" Before I can berate her further, a team of police storm the market. At least they're well dressed. The officers tackle me and drag me out of the store, screaming. A crowd is gathering as I'm thrown into the paddy wagon, and I *know* this mob is horribly dressed but because of the caged windows it's hard to be more precise.

I am in my cell now and am feeling better. Rehabilitated, I guess. Aretha Franklin is playing on the radio. True, she's the scariest-dressed celebrity in America, and I have all the pictures from *Jet* magazine to prove it, but I've learned in fashion therapy that she's so militant about her look that I have to love her for it. Even my numbered orange jumpsuit doesn't seem too terrible. My medication helps. If only my cellmate didn't have those stupid tattoos that everyone knows make any man over the age of thirty look worn-out no matter how masculine he was in his youth. I hope I don't have to kill him for it.

23

Independent Spirit Awards 2003

**(Delivered on March 22, one of the first days
after the United States started bombing Iraq)**

PART I

Well, someone once did call me the "Pope of Trash," but no one has ever called me an expert on world politics. So while I certainly have strong opinions of my own, I think I'll just thank you for joining us today in these scary times and welcome you to the Eighteenth Annual IFP/West Independent Spirit Awards.

Saddam Hussein, George Bush, NO ONE WILL STOP ME FROM GETTING MY GIFT BAG.

Before we start, I've got a beef. *Jackass: The Movie* was totally ignored here this year—not one single nomination! Yeah, I know the financing is MTV and Paramount, but so what? Call it a closet-independent film, and celebrate the hell out of it. *Jackass* was critic-proof, shot cheaply, made a fortune, and left audiences vomiting in the aisles. What more do you want? Its grossness, its grosses, and its greatness must never be forgotten!

Ah yes, I'm back. Have you noticed that all the other award shows are starting to look like the Independent Spirit Awards? Everything that gets nominated *is* an independent film. We're being co-opted. The studios churn out the romantic comedies and big-budget special effects movies to rake in the do-re-me, but we know what they really crave— *prestige*, and to win awards these days you gotta be dark. Maybe it's time the independent world gave the Hollywood "suits" some "notes" of our own on how to be successful.

Start with the writers. Hire low-priced first-time script doctors to make your mainstream movies less commercial— turn gold into silver. I'd love to get my hands on the next James Bond movie—John C. Reilly; "spilled, not shaken," Bjork as the love interest, and a title song by Old Dirty Bastard—and hey, you have a monster independent hit. Forget the standard "three acts" rule for the script: The hero has something, loses it, and gets it back in the third act while learning something. Let's *start* with the hero losing it, he or she *never* gets it back, and all the characters turn into drug addicts. Let 'em sing, too! Whoever thought one of my movies, *Hairspray,* could be turned into a hit Broadway musical? Well, it has, and now it's *Cats* for fat people!

Race as a profitable genre? Why not turn it around— switch the races of all the characters the day before you shoot. An all-white *Barbershop* would have to be seen to be believed, and an African-American *Sound of Music* might bring out a different kind of audience participation.

Lose dialogue altogether—Gus Van Sant pretty much did with *Gerry,* and he's got a "date movie" that only really smart girls put out for afterward. Todd Haynes channeled Douglas Sirk this year, but others have done it in the past; Woody Allen homaged Bergman; François Ozon did Fassbinder; how about Todd Solondz doing Preminger, or Oliver Stone *is* Russ Meyer?

Why hasn't anybody done a gay-related children's movie? Well, there was that Christmas film *Prancer* that sounded promising, but it didn't really deliver. Come on, gay people have more children than Catholics these days. Who's going to exploit their kids?—a whole new generation of sexual question marks. *Spider-Mary? Star Wars: Attack of the Castro Street Clones?* Both would work!

Of course sex still sells, but Hollywood, you have to confuse the MPAA with kinky sex acts that they can't rate NC-17. Spanking sure worked for Maggie Gyllenhaal this year. How about "sploshing"? The urge to dump food in your loved one's crotch—I'm not making this up—it's an English fetish. Meg Ryan? Sandra Bullock? Come on, you'd be great. "Adult Babies" might work, too. Have you seen the stories in the press about these guys? Grown men who eroticize being infants? Just think of the one-sheet. Mel Gibson, diapered in a bouncy chair with a hint of an erection—there's a surefire Independent Spirit Award winner!

Distribution heads, need help from the "specialized" world of independent film? If you already suspect your Hollywood film is going to tank *before* its release, don't dump it, lump it. Give out "flop" gift bags to all the V.I.P.s who attend the premiere. Just think what could be inside—oversized, outdated cell phones, a canned ham, stink bombs, Cindy Adams perfume, Delta Airlines bottled water, ugly publicity photos the star had supposedly "killed," and the bill from the studio for your limo ride home.

Stars—get creative, a bad dress is a good start, but you gotta do more these days. Arrive in style, but as I overheard a friend in New York say, "Limousines are soooo September tenth." Instead, *steal* a car, and have the police chase you here right up to the stage. You know how L.A. loves a car chase, and besides, all movie stars look more glamorous under arrest. *Everybody* knows that.

And to all the female beauties here today who work both sides of the Hollywood fence, I've got some advice—keep reinventing yourself to prove to the independent world that your heart really lies with us. Get reverse face-lifts to mock your Hollywood competition's fear of aging. Look older on purpose. Jennifer Aniston, add faux wrinkles. Parker Posey, sculpt on character-building bags under your eyes. Julianne Moore—grow a mustache, wear a fat-suit in your real life, admit Lillian Hellman looked her best the day before she died. And please, actresses: stop being nude at award shows! What's next on the red carpet? Featured "camel toes"? What happened to feminism? Does Brad show "plumber's crack" as he exits the stage? Of course not!

Technicians, you can help the studios be cooler, too! Labs, screw up—add a "hair in the gate" over the money shot and somebody will think it's intellectual. Sound men—let the microphone drop in frame right in a crucial scene, and you'll be invited to every film festival in the world. Camera men, make mistakes; soft focus, bad framing, jerky camera movement, none of this will hurt you—that's entertainment. Technique is nothing more than failed style. Wear your limitations with pride. If you want awards, somebody has to hate you—it might as well be the public.

PART II

I've got an idea—let's all sell out! Why not? Who needs credibility? To hell with art, let's get rich like everybody else in the movie business. Todd Haynes, want a second home in Malibu? Remake *Far from Heaven* for teenagers in the style of John Hughes—starring Britney Spears, "50 Cent" as the gardener, and Justin Timberlake as the confused boyfriend. And Miguel Arteta, in *The Good Girl*, Jennifer Aniston should have played every single part so she alone could have won the SAG award for best ensemble cast. And *Secretary II*, J-Lo! (*makes spanking motion*) WHACK! Need I say more?

I hate romantic comedies, but maybe I should try one anyway. Linda Hunt meets Philip Seymour Hoffman cute in

Baltimore—now that would be life-affirming in the independent sense of the word. Kids' movies usually make money, but children are such a tough audience these days. I asked an eight-year-old recently if he liked the *Wizard of Oz* and he said, "Not really, the *Wizard of Oz* is basically just walking." JUST WALKING!? Do you have to star Michael Jackson in your next movie to get this kid's attention? "Eat, Blanket, eat!"—it's not a bad ad campaign, and the words would look great on a child's lunchbox. (*looking into the camera*) Come on, "King of Pop," if you're out there watching, the independent film world awaits you. You've tried everything else, why not us? You're scary! Make a horror film! Just think of the trailer—(*imitates horror announcer*) "There's one thing wrong with Michael Jackson—HE'S ALIVE!" (*looking out into audience*) Bob Shaye, Mark Ordesky, forget *Lord of the Rings*. Let me direct it—*Freddy vs. Jason vs. Michael Jackson in Odorama!* It'll go through the roof!

PART III

(*After Foreign Film winner exits stage*)

Foreign films, I love those kind. I make foreign films myself, even here in my own country. I'm back again. I got a raise this year, so they're making me earn it. How can we make the Spirit Awards show better? If it ain't broke—don't fix it, right? I mean a film called *Dahmer* is nominated for the John Cassavetes Award here today—*what needs fixin'?!* Should we make the show longer, like our competitors? Pad it with clips from *The Piano Teacher* to weed out squeamish viewers and send them back to the networks where they belong? Should we feature dance numbers that weren't in the original film? Just think what a good choreographer and some chorus boys could do with *Narc*.

Maybe we need to be more aggressive in-house—punish and fine IFP members who don't send in their ballots. Lobby Landmark and Laemmle Theaters to admit all IFP voters free if they show their membership cards. Use Larry Clark's signature crotch-cam shots to liven up the excitement under the tables as the winners' names are read—maybe we already have! We're the lunatic fringe here today, and this show is our day pass from the mental institution known as the film biz. We're still afloat, and we're makin' movies—who needs FIX-ING?! We're the Spirit Awards!

PART IV

(Rejected by network)

Thank you. Well, I've done this show four years now, so maybe it's time to replace me. How about Johnny Knoxville next year as host—*Jackass*-style! "And the winner is . . . ahh-hhhh . . . a paper cut! As the tension builds, Johnny inserts the card with the winner's name into his rectum and fires out the award from his ass directly to the winner's table.

OK, John, get serious, here comes the big ones. To present the award for best director is ——.

PART IV

(Approved)

OK, here we go, it's time for the big ones—the awards that really count. Winners—I know that as soon as you hear your name called, you're secretly wondering, Does the Spirit Award mean my next salary will be higher? The answer is . . . no, and losers, well, try to pick up somebody backstage right afterward—a Spirit nomination is a terrible thing to waste.

24

If I Were President

Why should I elect you?
For the sheer perversity of it.

What would be your campaign slogan?
"Free Hairdos for the Poor."

How would you raise money for your campaign?
Auction off the vice presidency.

Which of your activities would present the greatest challenge to your spin doctors?
My fear of pets.

What activity would pose the biggest challenge to your Secret Service detail?
Flirting with criminals.

How much personal information do voters have the right to know about you?
Everything. Except my police record.

What's the biggest problem in the world? How would you fix it?
Racism. Forced primary residence swapping for one week a year to all citizens who live in racially segregated neighborhoods.

Whom would you appoint to your cabinet?
Gore Vidal, Ginny Foat, Angela Davis, Kweisi Mfume, Ramona Africa, Brooke Astor, Kitty Carlisle, and M. Jocelyn Elders.

Who would be your spiritual adviser?
   Phillip Berrigan (from beyond the grave).

Write the first news headline of your administration.
   "FILTH UPSET!!"

What person, living or dead, would you model yourself after as the leader of the free world?
   Shirley Chisholm.

What book would be required White House reading?
   The Lonely Lady of San Clemente: The Story of Pat Nixon by Lester David.

Whom would you pardon?
   Patricia Hearst, again and again. And I'd grant parole to Leslie Van Houten.

What would you legalize?
   An all-volunteer lesbian army.

What would you outlaw?
   Guns, New Age crystals.

What would you veto every time it hit your desk?
   Pro–death penalty legislation.

What would be your favorite presidential perk?
   Wild, daredevil, faux-kamikaze flights on *Air Force One*.

What three objects must you have in the Oval Office?
   An answering machine, a pen, and a manual for pushing the button to start nuclear war.

Who would get an invitation to stay in the Lincoln Bedroom?
   Jeff Stryker, Blaze Starr.

Who would never get an invitation?
   Colin Powell.

How would you unwind from the pressures of your job?
   Poppers.

Name the movie based on your presidency.
   Mondo Trasho II.